KEVIN CANFIELD

Mastering Sales

19 Years at the Intersection of Procter & Gamble and Walmart

By Kevin Canfield

Main Street Media USA
112 W Center St. Suite 410
Fayetteville, AR 72701

ISBN-13:978-1468099447

Contents

Acknowledgements

There are so many people to thank for contributing to my life, my career, and to this book, I almost hesitated to write this section for fear of offending someone that I may leave out, but I decided to proceed and apologize in the beginning to all that I don't properly recognize.

First, I must recognize the other original three members of the William Procter Sales Master group from North America; Jim Dobens, Jim Cannan, and Keith Johnson. The idea for this book was actually rooted in a meeting that we four had with Gary Cofer to identify ways that the WPSM's could have a bigger and more positive impact on P&G's entire sales organization and especially our new, young people. Keith and the Jim's were not only supportive of the concept, but also a source of encouragement and a reality check along the way. Thanks guys!

Next, I think I should recognize all of the people who have helped manage me over my 37 year career. To Terry Clampitt, Tom Osterman, Jim Hagen, Rich Gilchrist, Tom Obrien, Tom Muccio, Mike Russell, Tim Toll, Maria Edelson, and Steve Blair who have laughed, cried, screamed for joy and in exasperation as the occasion demanded and contributed to what I learned along the way. Thank you. Steve Blair should get some extra credit here. He was one of the first people to actually read the book and was quick to encourage its completion. He was also involved in the actual work at the end to get it printed and distributed. Thanks, Steve.

To the members of my respective teams who helped deliver all the results that I will discuss in this book and who have taught me so much about life, people, joy and laughter, I say thank you. From John Mannion and Armand Luzi to Joffrey Mendoza and Kevin Springate and everyone in between, I say thank you for giving me your best efforts and contributing to my success as well as the company's. No one can do it all by themselves.

Finally, to my families. Yes, I did use the plural here. I must thank the family of my birth for delivering me to adulthood, alive and with some sense of good and bad, right and wrong and with a proper perspective of the important things in life. Of course, it starts with Joe and Rita (my parents) who somehow guided seven children to adulthood without losing any and who stayed together for their entire marriage, not a small thing these days. Also, having five sisters will always keep your head on straight, and of course we all need one brother who you can throw up on (literally) and live to tell about it. Not that I don't still struggle every day to get it right, but any foundation I have is to their credit.

To the family that I created with my wife Brenda, I owe the biggest THANK YOU. Brenda and my two daughters, Stacey and Paige, have not only given me unquestioned support in every way, but also have taught me much about life, love, and the real joy that is available to all of us. You are the best thing that has ever happened to me and I should get down on my knees each day and give thanks for your presence in my life.

To all who have contributed to this book and to my life, I say THANK YOU.

A Living Document

There are really just two reasons why I set forth on this project. First, I have heard the advice many times that if you are going write about something for the first time, it is a good idea to write about what you know. The one thing you can say about this book is that it is what I know. It is my life, my career, my teams, my results, my experiences, my opinions, and my counsel. I think it is safe to say that I know about these things.

I have always said that I very rarely agree with anybody on everything, so if you are anything like me, you will probably not agree with every opinion in this book. That's OK. There are probably many opinions in this book that you *will* agree with, and even when you don't, hopefully this book will force you to think about and clarify your position. The second reason I wrote this book is to make you better at what you do and to get better – faster.

You may have read in the Acknowledgements that the genesis of this book was a desire by the four original North American members of the William Procter Sales Masters to have a positive impact on our sales people. Between the four of us we have over 100 years of experience. We have been successful, and we know what that looks like and what it takes. We have also seen failure, and we know what that looks like and we know what caused it. The question was, how could we share those experiences so that our new people could become successful more quickly and avoid some of the problems that we encountered. This book was just one of the ideas that we developed.

But, times change. I know that market conditions are different today than when I started with the company. I know that I have not been all-inclusive in terms of the skills that are important to be successful in sales at P&G. Also, I'm sure there are many other stories out there that can exemplify the skills and the business fundamentals discussed in this book. This is where the challenge comes in.

In order to make this book a living document and in the spirit of continual improvement, I encourage you to consider sending me suggestions for improvement after you have read it. Is there another skill that you would like to emphasize? Tell me about it. Tell me why it is important and how your personal use of that skill made you successful. Do you have your own story about one of the skills or business fundamentals that are already outlined in this book? Send it to me.

The goal of this challenge is to keep this book up to date AND to make it better. Hopefully, there will be multiple printings of this book and your contribution could appear in one of them. Please, take the challenge when you turn the last page and consider contributing to its content. The only thing that I can guarantee is that we will consider every submission. Send your ideas in. Get considered, and make this book better and even more relevant than it is today. Send your contributions to:

kkcbsu@cox.net

Introduction

Chapter 1

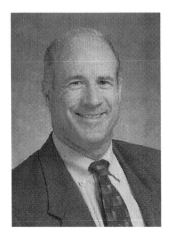

Kevin Canfield, author and

WPSM class of 2004

The first question you must ask yourself before you read this book is, "Who is Kevin Canfield, and why should I care what he knows about selling?" It would be fair for you to expect some good solid sales techniques along with years of practical experience. Even beyond theory and experience, it would be fair for you to expect some evidence that I have also been successful in all of those years of selling. Hopefully, this introduction will satisfactorily answer all of these questions and entice you to read on and learn how to be successful in selling, especially in Consumer Products.

Before I tell you all of the details about what has made me - me, I think I should give you some confidence that I have the three key qualities mentioned above.

1. Knowledge of the classic and currently accepted sales techniques.
2. Years of practical experience, and
3. Evidence of success or Mastery in Sales.

The short answer to how I satisfy these requirements is that I have worked for Procter & Gamble (possibly the best sales training company in the world) for 37 years and I am one of only nine sales people originally designated as a William Procter Sales Master. To quote the William Procter Sales Master award, this honor goes to,

> **"CBD career-coded managers, who have delivered sales mastery over a sustained period of time at the frontlines of our two most important interfaces – the daily work of building the business with our customers and building sales mastery with our people. CBD bestows this recognition to a highly select number of managers. Once received, the recognition will stay with the individuals for the balance of their career, carried as an additional title."**

The long answer starts in 1974!

After I graduated from Ball State University in Muncie, Indiana with a degree in Marketing, I went right to work for Procter & Gamble. At that time Procter & Gamble was recognized as one of the finest selling companies in the world, and that fact is still true today. As I suggested above, I could argue that P & G was also one of, if not THE, best sales training companies anywhere at that time. Let me give you a quick look at what training looked like for P&G back in 1974. As you'll see, training back then was intense and complete.

Knowledge of Sales Techniques

After a week of working with my unit manager, and slowly moving from watching him sell to doing the selling myself, I was thrust out into the world of retail stores to sell and learn from my successes and failures for about six months. In those days we were expected to visit 11 to 12 stores every day and try to sell three to four displays or other ideas on each call. You can do the math. I was making three selling presentations in 11 stores every day for about 230 days per year (work days minus estimated meeting days). That's a rate of almost 8,000 selling presentations per year! There is a lot of learning that happens in all of those calls. You learn about people, and you learn about techniques that work, and don't work.

After about six months, or about 4,000 selling situations, I was sent to a weeklong selling school in Cincinnati where I was exposed to the latest selling and communications techniques. They showed us how to sell with the Persuasive Selling Format, which we will talk about later. They showed us how to handle objections with communications techniques such as the DUVH model (Determine, Understand, Verify and Handle). The timing was perfect. After six months of banging my head against a wall and making all kinds of mistakes, this formal training really made sense.

Now that I was armed with some solid techniques, P&G sent me back out in the world for another year and a half of sales immersion. I was still learning every day, but now I was learning more from my successes than my failures.

Years of Practical experience

After two years of this selling science lab, I was promoted to a Unit Manager position where I trained people like me AND managed the major accounts in a given geography. My geography ended up being in Pittsburgh, Pennsylvania. Unit Managers back then handled major account headquarters like Kroger, Safeway, Albertson's, etc. My largest major account was a wholesaler named Charley Brothers, which supplied the Shop 'n' Save stores in the Pittsburgh area. Of course, with only a few headquarter accounts to sell, the number of presentations I had to prepare and deliver went way down, but the consequences of those presentations were of much greater magnitude!

Charley Brothers was one of the most difficult accounts in the Pittsburgh District. For whatever reason, it seemed that the actual Charley brothers just didn't like P&G very much. This, actually, was not that uncommon back then. We had some great brands and had our way of doing things. We weren't always the most flexible company to work with, but we were as fair as any company could be. I shipped my quota every year in Pittsburgh despite managing this difficult account, and I must have gained a reputation as a bit of a "turn around" artist, because over the last few years in Pittsburgh I was assigned three other "difficult" accounts. In each case I was able to make significant breakthroughs and, despite the challenge, did in fact continue to ship quota.

After Pittsburgh, I was promoted to District Manager in San Francisco. In that role I didn't even manage an account in the beginning. My job was to manage people. It was to direct, enable, and motivate those people. Now, you're probably saying, "Wow, that's a little silly! Why would P&G move their best sales people out of selling assignments as they promoted them into management?" If you were thinking that, then you should feel pretty smart, because that is exactly what P&G was thinking. In the late 80's and the early 90's, P&G started moving to a "Customer Team" concept. That meant that these teams would be centered around the Customers (like Safeway, Albertson's, etc.) instead of geographies. It also meant that many of the previous District Managers would be put back in selling roles at the key accounts. When that happened, I went to the Walmart Team.

Evidence of Success

"OK!" you say. "Got it!" And, for some of you, just the mention of Walmart might be enough for you to start listening. As you might think, most companies send their very best people to manage their Walmart business, if for no other reason than it is a HUGE business. I would hope that is why P&G selected me to go to Arkansas. But just getting there is not enough. EXCELLING while you are there is what makes the difference.

When I got to the Walmart Team in 1991, I was asked to manage P&G's Beauty Care business. Beauty Care was made up of our Hair Care business which included Head & Shoulders and Pantene, our Deodorant business with Sure, Secret and Old Spice, and our Skin Care business which included our Olay and Noxzema brands. Over the next four years I more than tripled the size of that business, and, more importantly, built our brand shares relative to the rest of the United States. This is a very important measure, because it indicates success even after you factor in Walmart's considerable growth. During those four years, I earned recognition as being in the top 1 to 2 percent of P&G's sales force, and in the fourth year, I was awarded P&G's Chairman's Club award given to P&G's top performers. This is a little bit more of an indication that I know how to sell at the highest levels and that I might be worth listening to, but there's more.

After my time managing the Beauty Care Business, P&G President and Team Leader, Tom Muccio, asked me to go over and manage our Food and Beverage Business. This business was in distress, and according to Tom, it needed a savvy, top-notch manager to handle the business for a couple of years. This was the first time that Tom referred to me as his, "Big right hander from the Bullpen". This was a huge compliment from Tom, and helped me understand that I was beginning to earn a reputation on the Walmart Team similar to the one I had earned in Pittsburgh. It was an energizing feeling.

The Food and Beverage business WAS in distress, but despite that, I was able to ship our objective both years that I was there. That's when Tom came back and asked me to take on one more challenge. Our Oral Care business was under assault by Colgate. Our shares were down, and Colgate actually had a product technology edge that needed to be overcome. To make things worse, Walmart's profitability on our Oral Care business was not good, to put it mildly. The good news was that we had a strong pipeline of new product initiatives that were ready to be launched. These product initiatives were a mixed blessing. New is always good, but new item launches require hard work, experience, and of course, excellent selling skills. Tom wanted me to guide our Oral Care business through these challenging yet opportunistic times.

Over the next four years we were able to launch nine major product initiatives and almost tripled the size of that business. As with the Hair Care business, we grew shares relative to our total US business, which is the real measure of success on the Walmart team. Amazingly, we were able to do this while improving Walmart's profitability on our brands at the same time. Now, I think I may have said that too fast. P&G's business got significantly bigger (which usually means that the business gets more competitive which leads to profit pressure) and Walmart's profitability went up. What's wrong with this picture – NOTHING! It is an amazing story, which we will get into with more detail later.

WILLIAM PROCTER SALES MASTER

By this time I had 30 years of experience, selling at the highest level at probably the best Sales Company in the world. It was at this time that P&G decided to reward/honor their very best people by creating an elite society called the William Procter Sales Masters, in honor of P&G's first salesman, William Procter. As of the writing of this book, there are only nine people in the world in this group, and only four in North America. And, as I told you earlier, I'm one of them. Now, if you had any doubt up until now if I were worth listening to, I would hope that this would push you over the edge. Should you listen to one of the best sales people from one of the very best sales companies in the world if you want to learn how to sell? I think the answer is yes!

Not only do I know how to sell, but I think I can teach you how to do it as well. What you learn will be a combination of what Procter and Gamble teaches their new sales people and what I have experienced over 30 years selling to everyone from store managers to the top executives at the largest retailer in the world. If you sell for a living this could have a HUGE impact on your results and your life. Even if you don't sell for a living, we all need to be persuasive at times in our life, and this book will help you do that like a professional.

So, read on and learn the secret to being persuasive and influential in your personal life and how to be successful in your sales life. You will learn the thought process and delivery format that will make all of your proposals more likely to be "bought" or accepted. You'll emerge more persuasive, more successful, and consequently, better at what you do!

What We Do And How We Do It

Chapter 2

Throughout my working life, friends and family have asked me, "What do you do for a living?" I usually start by saying that I work for Procter & Gamble, but they eventually have to ask me exactly what do I do for P&G. So, I would tell them that I sell Pantene or Secret Deodorant or Crest Toothpaste to whatever customer I happen to be responsible for at the time. Inevitably they say, "Wow, that sounds like an easy job. Who couldn't sell Crest Toothpaste to (Fill in a retailer name here)?" As you might imagine, this only got worse when I started calling on Walmart. "Who couldn't sell Crest Toothpaste to Walmart? Don't they have to buy Crest?"

The worst part of these conversations is that the answer to that last question is, kind of, Yes! P&G does a great job of creating demand for the products we sell, so people think that I can just lay on the couch all day and wait for Walmart to call me with orders to replace the product that shoppers bought at their stores. That would probably be a true picture if it weren't for those pesky competitors. Walmart competes with other retailers for their business, and P&G competes with other manufacturers for its business. It is this competition that brings the challenge to our jobs.

I don't think that this will come as a shock to anyone, but I believe my first responsibility is to P&G. My job is to make sure that our brands win at the customers for whom I am responsible versus our competition, the Colgates, Unilevers and Kimberly Clarks of the world. And, of course, those other companies have people who are supposed to make sure that their brands win versus P&G. We are constantly competing for the limited attention and resources of the retailers. These retailers (even Walmart) have limited warehouse space to carry items everyday. They have a finite amount of shelf space, which they can devote to these items in their stores, and they have a limited amount of display space (endcaps, aisle displays, etc) which they can use to "promote" manufacturers' brands. The battle for this attention and resources can be fierce! So, given this environment, what exactly is our job?

My very first manager at P&G defined the responsibility of a sales person at P&G about as well as a person can. I've heard other people try to capture the essence of my job through the years, but none have been better. Here is what he said,

> "Our job is to place our brands in front of the shopper in the most appealing way possible through the four Business Fundamentals:
>
> -Distribution
> -Pricing
> -Shelf Management
> -Merchandising (Feature and Display)"

In Sales (or Customer Business Development – CBD) we can influence a product's packaging, its pricing and even its performance, and the good sales people do that. However, those

> # Sales of any kind
> # is part Art
> # and part Science

things are not our primary responsibility. Our job is to make sure that our brands look as good as possible at store level, where the shopper often makes her decision on what to buy, at what we call the First Moment of Truth (FMOT). R&D, Manufacturing and Marketing create great products that perform well at the Second Moment of Truth (at home usage) and create the initial demand for those products with the shopper. That is their job, their primary responsibility. They, especially Marketing or the GBU at P&G, can have an influence on how those products will look at store level, but that is not their job. That is MY job. Go back to the definition above. I think it is the best, cleanest, most accurate definition of the sales job in the consumer goods business.

Earlier, I mentioned that my primary responsibility has always been to The Company, P&G. Now, we must talk about a very strong, while secondary, responsibility that I always felt that I had, and that is to the customer that I serviced. I have always felt that I had the duty to figure out how my customer could use my brands to achieve their goals. Retailers need customers, volume, profit, efficiencies in labor and inventory and more. Luckily for me, P&G offers strong brands that can deliver on virtually all these needs, even profitability. But, you can't sell profitability if the retailer needs volume and customers and vice versa. You really need to understand your customer in order to position your brands to satisfy their needs.

The purpose of this book is to help you become more successful at selling, in general, but in the consumer products business more specifically. I recently addressed a group of college students as part of an orientation to P&G and the Walmart Team. At the end of my talk, we allowed the students to ask any questions they might have. One student raised her hand and said, "I understand how big P&G is and what a great company it is, but what I really want to know is, how does anyone become successful in sales at P&G." This was a great question, I thought, especially since she knew that she was talking to a William Procter Sales Master. I wanted to give her a good answer, so I thought hard about it, and answered her question something like this:

> "Sales of any kind, but particularly at P&G, is part art and part science. The artist in me sees the Customer (the Retailer) as his or her canvas and the four Business Fundamentals as their brushes or tools. Upon the canvas we all apply different combinations (or shades) of skills and personal qualities with our tools to deliver a result, a painting if you will, of our subject - the Brands we sell."

While all sales people at P&G have the same subject matter (our brands), the quality of the painting can be vastly different from one retailer to the next, depending on the receptiveness of the canvass and the combination of skills and personal qualities we have applied, hopefully, with the appropriate brushes. In every retailer, you will find our brands in different locations on the shelf, with different pricing strategies and with different levels of merchandising support. All of this is a reflection of the talent of the artful sales person.

The science part of sales is like a doctor with a patient. As a sales person, you will always have a sea of data at your disposal. To be a good doctor, you need to sort through all of this information to identify the pieces that are important to your patient, the retailer. You can't diagnose the patient unless you have read the data properly, and you can't help the patient (prescribe the proper treatment or strategy) unless your diagnosis is on target. In this analogy, once you have the proper diagnosis, you can operate on the patient with your surgical tools, the Business Fundamentals.

Whether you lean toward art or science, this book will help you understand your canvas or patient, your tools and the key skills and qualities that you need to paint your brands in their most favorable light.

We will talk about each of the business fundamentals and discuss why each is important. I will also give you examples of what I believe are the most important skills and personal qualities that you need to ensure that you are as successful as you can possibly be, and that you deliver the sales. In short, so that you can sell!

Introduction for Persistence by Sylvain Benoit,

William Procter Sales master – class of 2006

Introduction:

Tenacity, determination, perseverance and hard work are words that we have heard before in our CBD environment, right? They are words that are synonymous with persistence and are music to my ears.

Persistence is a unique, fundamental quality that every individual should have to be successful in a competitive environment. In my view, if I did not have this quality built into my personality, I would have never known the feeling that I get when I deliver on one of my commitments. It is doing everything you can to achieve whatever you have committed to. The more difficult it is to achieve, the better you feel once you have delivered on it.

NEVER GIVE UP on something that you commit to. It is all about the pride you generate once you have achieved it.

Persistence

Chapter 3

I think it was Woody Allen who said, "90% of success is showing up". In other words, if you just show up every day on your job and show up to address all of your challenges, you are 90% of the way to success. I am a huge believer in that adage. From my earliest days, I always showed up. Even though my father always told me, "never say never", I'm going to say that I never skipped practice in any sport in which I played, and when I got into any game, I NEVER wanted to come out. In college, I NEVER skipped classes, and when I was in class I always paid attention and took good notes. Now, was I the best athlete in my High School? Hardly, but by the time I graduated, I won all conference and all state honors, received a college scholarship to play football and I'm currently in the Indiana Football Hall of Fame. Since I have already admitted that I was not even the best athlete in my high school, I have to attribute any success that I had largely to my persistence.

In college, I was also not the brightest bulb on campus, but by the time I graduated, I qualified for Academic All-American nomination. As I stated above, I did this by showing up everyday for class and taking good notes. In other words, I even "showed up" when I showed up. I don't have to guess what led to my good grades. It was my persistence that made the difference.

If you talked to any of the people who had the dubious honor to manage me throughout my career, I think they would all agree that my "persistence" was at least one of the keys to my success. I have been called a pit bull and a wirehaired terrier with a tennis ball by my managers and a pain in the ---- by my competition. I was "Die Hard" before it became a movie, and this was actually a good thing. There are some "watch outs" if this is a natural characteristic of yours, and I will talk about that at the end of this chapter, but for now, let's focus on the positive aspects of persistence.

Before I talk to you about my personal experiences with persistence, I would like to tell you about two Sales Reps that worked for me while I was a Unit Manager in the Pittsburgh District (the old world of P&G). Their names were John Manion and Armand Luzi, and they could not have been more different.

John was the stereotypical Irish pub dweller. John always had a song in his heart and a joke on his lips and a prank up his sleeve. The first day that I worked with John, we were scheduled to call on a small chain food store, which he sold direct. He told me it was going to be a tough call and wanted to prepare me for the worst. As we walked into the store, an announcement came over the PA system, "Will the greatest sales person in the world, John Manion, please report to the manager's office." This demonstrated two things about John. First, he was a world-class prankster to do this to his unit manager on their first day together. Second, this account loved John and he had significant influence with the owner and managers. Why?

Armand Luzi couldn't have been more different. Armand was a plodder. If he were a football team, he would have been Ohio State under Woody Hayes – Three yards and a cloud of dust. If he were a philosophy, he would be, "A penny saved is a penny earned." And if he were a character in a fable, he would be the tortoise in "The Tortoise and the Hare".

> # 90% of success
> # is just showing up!

The first call I made with Armand was at one of his biggest direct accounts called Pechin's. This was a very unusual account, but I will try to describe it as one of the first Supercenters that sold everything from clothes to HABA (Health & Beauty Aids). They also had their own cafeteria that sold discount meals to the elderly (and just plain cheap to everyone else). They had part of their back room in a cave, but they sold a LOT of HABA at very good prices. When Armand walked in, he said a few words to the department manager, and then rolled up his sleeves and started building displays all over the store with product he had ordered the last time he was there. In the end we had pulled out over 100 cases of product and put them on an assortment of displays. By the end of this first call, I knew this account loved Armand, and he had significant influence with the owner and managers. Why?

Note, that the last sentence about Armand and the last sentence about John Manion are the same; how could that be? They are SO different. They couldn't possibly have anything in common. But they did have one thing in common. They were persistent. They showed up everyday and their customers knew that they could count on them, and they did! Both were wildly successful and wildly different, but both had that one quality in common. The point to this story is that you don't have to look the same to be persistent. You can still be you, whoever that is, add persistence and you will become a better version of yourself.

While this is a little off the subject, there is one story that I have to tell about Armand and John that will tell you a little more about both of them, and hopefully give you a little chuckle. Back in the old days we used to have Unit Meetings about once a month, usually at my house, to discuss our current objectives and our progress against them. At one of these such meetings, Armand was sitting at my dining room table, which is where we held our meetings, and he was playing with a rubber band (my meetings were always riveting). He was stretching it, and looking down the length of the rubber band to check for flaws in the manufacturing (this is my only guess), when it slipped out of his fingers and he shot himself in the eye.

Armand, as you might expect, leaped backwards out of his chair and bounced off of my dining room wall. Of course, to the rest of us, this looked a little spastic, since we had no idea what had just happened, except for John. They kept this little secret for years. Armand, because he was too embarrassed to tell me about it, and John, because he was, in effect, blackmailing Armand. As I look back at it, I should have known that something was up. Armand became VERY supportive of whatever stance John was taking on almost every issue. As different as they were, I should have known that it wasn't just like-mindedness. One day we were discussing a very import strategic choice for the unit (I'm sure) and Armand was opposing John's position, until I notice John toss a rubber band in front of Armand. Armand stared at the rubber band for a couple of seconds and promptly did a 180-degree turn on the issue. That's when I finally found out the whole story and also how John had been taking advantage of it for years.

If there is a point to that story it is: "Don't take yourself too seriously and forget to enjoy life as it races past you."

So, let's get back to persistence. There are three things you need to do to qualify for the title of "wire haired terrier with a tennis ball", and they all revolve around resisting temptation. If you want to be persistent, you must resist the temptation to:

1. Quit when things get tough.
2. Avoid doing the things you find unpleasant.

3. Rationalize that what you are doing is fine, even when you know in your heart that it is wrong.

First, Don't Quit!

You've heard the old saying that, "Quitters never win and winners never quit." Now, applying my father's old adage to this statement, I might not be able to defend the second half of that saying, but I'm pretty sure I can support the first half. I am sure that there are some great people out there, whom we would all classify as winners, who have quit at something in their lives. It is tough not to.

However, when you say, "Quitters never win", that probably IS true. It is similar to the golfing adage that says, "Never up, never in". This refers to a golfer's putting game and is saying that if you leave your putt short, you can never make it. You could have the line right (putt in the right direction, for you non-golfers) but if you do not get the ball to the hole, you can never make the putt. Quitting is very similar. It is stopping before you get to your goal or target. It is intentionally falling short of your best effort to reach a goal. If you stop before you win, I think it is safe to say that you can't possibly win. No matter how you slice it, I think it is safe to say that, "quitters never win". Sorry dad!

Let me tell you a personal story about "not" quitting. If you read the "Shelf" chapter, you will learn that one of my first and maybe finest shelf sales was at an account called Charley Brothers in Pittsburgh, PA. About a year before that successful story started, Charley Brothers actually asked to have me replaced as their account handler. I don't even remember the specific problem, but I do remember it had to do with me enforcing one of our company policies. I know it is hard to believe, but Charley Brothers did not like some of our policies.

> **Never say never, but quitters actually never win!**

After receiving their request, my District Manager actually asked me if I wanted to give Charley Brothers to another Unit Manager to diffuse the situation. I said, and I am quoting now, "ABSOLUTELY NOT!!!" As I look back at it, I think both my District Manager and the account expected me to step aside, but I wouldn't. In fact, I went to the account and told them that nothing would change, but that I was determined to give them the best service they would get from any vendor, AND I was going to enforce P&G policies! I think I won the respect of my District Manager with this decision, and, at a minimum, I shocked the account into a working relationship. Remember, this was the account that would supply my biggest shelf win just a year or so later. Certainly, in this case, it appears that I made the right decision.

As Winston Churchill said in 1941 as he addressed Harrow School, "never give in, never give in, never, never, never, never-in nothing, great or small, large or petty - never give in except to convictions of honor and good sense." I obviously agree with this statement. While it might be tempting to take the easy road in the short term (it certainly would have been easier for me to give up Charley Brothers) it is better to hang in there in the long term. People may not LIKE you for it, but they will respect you.

Second, Don't Avoid

There are many aspects to selling, some of which I really love. I love to analyze a situation and develop a plan to either fix it or exploit it, depending on what I find. I love to create the presentations that will eventually be used to "sell" whatever concept I've decided upon as a result of my analysis. I also love the give and take of the account call when I deliver that presentation. Now, all I have to do is find a job that only requires me to do those duties.

Unfortunately, every sales job that I have had or heard about would require me to do some things that I hate!! I hate, for example, the details of filling out paper work for the executional part of whatever I have sold. I also hate writing letters to my own company explaining what I did and how great it was or why my business is doing whatever it is doing. I would much rather live in a verbal world where none of this paperwork is necessary, but I don't.

Because I live in the real world that requires these things, I have decided to confront it and not avoid it. There is no award on my wall that says that I am the best "deal sheet filler outer" or the best "recommendation writer", but I can tell you that I have worked hard at both of these things, despite that fact that I don't particularly like to do either.

I can't tell you how to excel in all of the areas that you hate to perform in, because those areas are different for all of us. I can tell you two things, however. First, every job has those unlikable duties. I know doctors who love to be in the operating room, but hate to deal with their patients after the surgery, and vice versa. I know sales people who actually don't like the selling environment, but are successful because they do the other things very well and work at the selling part with all their effort. There is no such thing as the perfect job.

Second, I **can** tell you what will happen if you go the extra mile and work on all of the "not fun" things you have to do. You will be viewed as a complete sales person and you will have plenty of plaques on your wall. These plaques won't talk about all the little things you did that you hated. They will simply say, "This person was the best!" He or she did it all, and did it well. None of Larry Bird's awards say that he hustled after every loose ball, and boxed out on every rebound, but he did, and that is

> **"Never give in;**
>
> **Never give in,**
>
> **Never, never, never**
>
> **Give in."**
>
> **Winston Churchill**

what make him great! You can be the Larry Bird of selling if you do it all, all the time, with all your best effort.

Third, Don't Rationalize

Now, I know I started this chapter with a Woody Allen saying, but I'm going to have to risk quoting Woody twice inside these few pages. This quote just fits too well. It was Woody who said, "no one can get through even one day without at least one good rationalization." That may be true, but it is a sad statement about all of us. For me, this most often shows up when I ignore feedback from my bosses, peers and sometimes even the customer. It is so easy for me to say, "Those guys don't know me! They don't have a clue of what I'm all about. I know me a lot better than they could possibly know me."

It is true that no one is closer to you than you, but rationalizing in any way will make you appear out of touch with reality. In the case of feedback, even if people are wrong, their comments represent how they see you. Right or not, it is their perception of you and you need to deal with it.

Finally, I should talk a little about the negative aspect of persistence and how you can avoid that downside. If you have ever played "fetch" with a wirehaired terrier (which I have been called), you know that the first few times when he won't let go of that ball, you might think it is cute or you might even be impressed with his (or her) tenacity. About the fourth or fifth time, you begin to say things like, "let go of the ---- ball, you idiot!" and not long after that, the game will be over. I guess that would say that persistence or tenacity, while a good trait, can also get on anyone's nerves if it is overdone.

I must admit that I could have a tendency to overdo my persistence, falling on my sword over every issue, which could be as painful as it sounds for me and for all around me. If you would like to keep the positive aspects and benefits of being persistent but avoid the downside, I have found that there are three things that will help:

1. **Slow down your reaction time** – I'm sure you've heard the advice that when you write a letter in anger, you should put it in your drawer for at least a day, and the reread it before you send it. Whenever I have done that, I have always dramatically changed

the letter or decided not to send it at all. You can do the same with your verbal responses. When you feel that uncontrollable urge to argue over some issue, hold yourself back. Sometimes this may only take a few minutes or even seconds. While you are holding yourself back think about the other people around you. What are their positions on the issue? How might they take your dissension? Can you soften your approach? As I have aged and employed this strategy, I have found that while I participate in fewer debates, because I decide to avoid some, I actually win over more people, more often. This approach takes discipline and practice, but trust me, it pays off.

2. **Praise in public and criticize in private** – This one is easy. We all can see how it works for us. I personally don't mind being praised in public and I really hate being criticized in front of a crowd of people. DUH! Despite that, I'm amazed at how often I have challenged people in front of a group, even my bosses. Now, think about it. If a peer doesn't like to be criticized in front of a crowd, how do you think your manager is going to respond if you criticize him or her in front of their own team? Even if you are right, your chance to positively influence anyone goes WAY down. Write your point down and approach your manager after the meeting! You'll do less damage, and your chance to influence the situation goes WAY up!

3. **Listen to your broad-based feedback** – I used to take feedback like a man going through a trunk in the attic. What I liked, I kept, and what I didn't like, I threw out. This habit is very closely related to the "rationalization" problem that we discussed earlier. It may have made me feel better, but it didn't help me **become** better. The reality is, what people think IS what they think. It might even be off base, but it is what they think. Listen to what they say and then figure out if this is an actual problem that you have to fix or if it is a perception that you have to change. I think you will find that, either way, the plans that you will need to put together to resolve the issue will be the same or at least very similar.

If you are able to add these three ingredients to your persistent character you will be a manager's dream. I call it, "having persistence with judgment." You will have the tenacity that all managers love to see in their people, but it will be softened by a judgment that helps you know when and where to use it.

Now, I'm sure that all of my previous managers will say that they have already given me this advice. That's possible. I was soooo busy gnawing on that tennis ball that I may have missed it. I wish I would have learned it sooner. I'm sure it would have positively impacted my career and life, and it can do the same for you.

If you learn this lesson now, people will just respond better to you. You'll be like that energetic, tenacious wirehaired terrier that has also learned how to play fetch sometimes. Not all the time, just some times! Because people (your people, your managers, even your customers) actually like you more, you'll find that you will get more things done, and you will be more successful.

> **Persistence with judgment, the perfect formula**

And if you are more successful, you'll be happier! Take it from a terrier that learned the "fetch" game late in life. You'll have to give up the ball every once in a while, but if you do, more people will be willing to play! Give it a try!

Introduction for Merchandising by Jim Waugh,

William Procter Sales master – class of 2006

Introduction:

The conversation around features and displays is critically important, impacting both the shopper and retailer. The impact is both economic and image. Today's shopper is quite astute, constantly examining the 'value' equation of not just a specific product, but also a specific retailer. Brand names are powerful – they have an image that draws people to them. Likewise, shoppers also have an image of a given retailer. Featuring leading brands creates a positive impression or image in the shopper's mind – they carry the brand I like and at a 'fair' price. As a shopper, however, the most frustrating event is to arrive at your store of choice only to find that the advertised brand is out-of-stock! Shoppers don't want a 'rain check' or a like product! Often, I have walked out of a store because they were out-of-stock. Preventing out-of-stocks is the most compelling reason to display a product! It is extremely difficult to measure the negative impact, at the retail level, from either an image or economic measure when out-of-stocks occur. The bottom line is this: Surround the customer with the brands they want ... and they will return. Be bold in proclaiming this message – Displays are bold and reduced price displays are the ultimate way to surround your customers.

Merchandising

(Display and Featuring)

Chapter 4

You would think that something as basic as "The Business Fundamentals" in consumer product sales would not change, thus the name! That would just go to show you that nothing stays the same, not even the fundamentals. In 1974, when I started with P&G, there were actually five Business Fundamentals. Since I started in the Health and Beauty Aids division, we called these fundamentals the five fingers of HABA. They were:

- -Distribution
- -Pricing
- -Shelf Management
- -Feature, and
- -Display

Today, we talk about <u>four</u> Business Fundamentals. Somewhere in the last 30 years P&G has consolidated the last two fundamentals (Feature and

Display) into one called Merchandising. You should know that I really prefer the old designation to the new, and you are probably saying, "That's just because you are old and don't like change and you simply prefer things to be the way they used to be." While I am old and sometimes prefer things to be the way they used to be, I almost always have a very good reason for my preference. In this case, I think we have combined two Business Fundamentals that have totally different purposes into one, and I'm actually not sure why.

Let's talk about Featuring. This is when the retailer runs an ad in the paper or in their circular, or roto, or whatever. The purpose of this ad is to bring people into a retailer's stores. They want to tell people who are sitting at home about the great deals they have in their stores and entice them to come in and buy them. Featuring is all about traffic, and that is an important objective for most retailers. If a retailer believes that they already have enough shoppers in their stores, they should eliminate their featuring or at least reduce it significantly.

Now you ask, "What retailer believes they already have enough shoppers in their stores? Aren't they all trying to draw more people in?" While most retailers are looking to get more shoppers in their stores, others do not struggle as much with this problem. Walmart, for example, has over a 100 million people coming through their stores each week, and with this traffic comes many challenges. In-stock, cleanliness and speed through the cash registers, etc. are all real issues for them. Many of their stores are very crowded and they really don't need many more shoppers in those stores. They really just need to sell more to the people who are already there, and that is where the Display Business Fundamental comes in. They have, consequently, reduced their featuring significantly. While most retailers run weekly ads, Walmart runs only one ad per month. They would run even less, and eliminate the expenses associated with that kind of advertising, but I think they see their monthly ads as a minimum outreach to their customers to keep Walmart "top of mind" when they are planning their shopping trips.

Display, by its nature, does not bring new customers into any store. It is already "in" the store, so people have to come into the store to even experience it. Display can, however, be very effective at selling more to any store's existing shoppers. It can remind them of what they need but forgot to put on their shopping list. It can entice them to buy something that they don't necessarily need, but want. It can trade them up to a more expensive item or a bigger size. No matter which of these things it does, display can sell your shoppers more, and that is a good thing.

Is Merchandising the most important Business Fundamental?

In the chapter on Distribution, I will walk you through a discussion of which of the Business Fundamentals is the most important. The argument for Distribution is, "If you don't carry it, you can't sell it." The argument for shelf is that 80-90% of our volume is done off the shelf, so Shelf must be the most important. I guess it's all about how you measure importance.

> # Merchandising –
> # the icing on a
> # great business cake!

If you measure importance by the amount of time we devote to it, then Merchandising will win this argument hands down. When I was managing the Oral Care business for the Walmart team, I would estimate that at least 50% of my time was spent on activities related to selling Walmart merchandising. Whether that activity was creating presentations to sell Walmart on why they should merchandise my brands or forecasting the eventual volume back to Cincinnati or making sure that volume actually shipped as planned, merchandising takes up much of a sales person's time.

Merchandising also delivers that EXTRA business that can really make the difference between a good year and a great one. It may only represent only 10-20% of your volume, but who would want to give that up. Anyone who has tracked a Consumer Products business has seen and felt the impact of a good Feature and or Display. Who would want to miss out on an event that can sell two to five weeks of volume in just one week? Below is an example of a business that has had some merchandising events run against it. I've taken away the brand names and disguised the actual volume, but I think you can easily pick out the weeks that had merchandising attached to them. This should give a good sense of why sales people want as much of this kind of support as they can get, within reason.

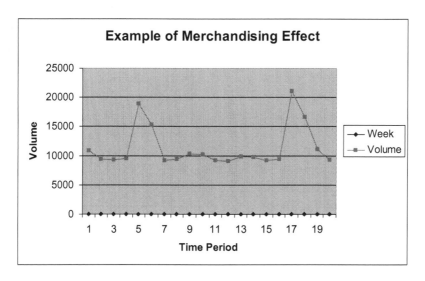

Merchandising is truly the icing on a great business cake. A good display and feature can easily double a brand's volume for the first week that it hits the stores, and it can have a positive lingering effect even in the second or third weeks that it is in the stores. Think of it this way, if you were to sell even four events a year, and each event delivered an extra week and a half's worth of business, that's an extra six weeks of volume in a 52 week year. That's almost 12% more business than a year with no merchandising. That's why we all want as much feature and display support as we can get, but be careful, once you have a good merchandising year, it becomes your base for the next year. Then, you have to match your merchandising support from the previous year to just break even. It can be like a drug. It is definitely addicting.

Sounds a little like a rat race doesn't it? Why don't we just skip the merchandising fundamental all together and make it easier on ourselves every year? The answer is that merchandising drives share, and if your retailer is going to merchandise your category, then you have to make sure you are getting your fair share of the merchandising or your overall share will suffer. If you don't get your fair share that means your competitor is getting it, and I think we all know that can *not* be good. The key is getting your fair share.

Now, here's a trick question. How do you calculate your fair share of merchandising? You would think that you should calculate it the same way you calculate fair share of shelf, right? Wrong! The thing you must remember about the shelf is that all brands that your retailer carries must be carried on the shelf so they must occupy some shelf space. In other words, every brand "participates" on the shelf. So, for the shelf it is proper to roughly give each brand its fair share of the shelf. If a brand represents 30% of a category's volume, then it should occupy about 30% of that category's shelf space. This is just good business. We'll explain this in more detail in the Shelf Management chapter, but for now I think we can instinctively agree with this concept.

When it comes to merchandising, however, there are some brands that will NEVER be merchandised, because they are just too small. Maybe the best way to illustrate how to calculate your fair share of merchandising is through an example.

Let's say that you have a category that has ten brands competing for the volume. The biggest brand in the category is yours, and it represents 30% of the category's business. There is one competitive brand that represents 20% of that category's business and two other competitive brands that represent 10% of the volume. These four brands will definitely receive merchandising support. The remaining six brands in the category range from a 7% share to a 3% share and will never be featured because they are just too small.

Let's say that your retailer is going to run 10 merchandising events in this category next year. How many events should your brand receive? You would think three, right? (30% of 10 events = 3 events). Wrong! Since only 70% of your retailer's volume will be merchandised, that 70% becomes your total universe, so your brand actually has a 43% share of the brands that will be merchandised (30% divided by 70% = 43%). Your brand should receive at least four of the 10 events next year, not three!

You might be saying, "What's the big deal? It's just one extra event!" Well, when one event can deliver 2 to 3% of incremental annual business, each event is a big deal, and it is important that you get it instead of your competition. It should also be important to your retailer. They should want to ensure they are merchandising the right brands with the right frequency. Over merchandising smaller brands can cause them to under deliver on their goals and flood their stores with unproductive inventory.

Despite the fact that I argued earlier in this chapter that Display and Feature are very different, I must admit that they go together like ham and eggs. I believe, for example, that every feature should be supported by a display at store level for at least two reasons.

1. **To ensure in-stock** – The last thing any retailer wants to do is to draw a customer into their store with a featured item and then not have that item available when that customer gets there. At one time retailers might have actually employed a "bait and switch" strategy with their feature items, but I think that today everyone agrees that it is more important to provide a positive shopping experience than it is to try to manipulate their shoppers into buying something they don't want or need.

2. **To emphasize the message** – If an item is important enough to run in a retailer's ad, then you want to make sure that your shoppers get reminded of that message when they get to the store. Whether it is just the item that is important (maybe it's a new item) or the price, or a combination of those factors, it is important to reinforce that message to your customers when they are in your store.

Personally, I think that display is a more effective merchandising vehicle than feature. In other words, I believe that display simply sells more product than featuring. I base this on personal experience and the Popai-Dupont study on display and featuring that is over 30 years old, but is still the only accepted study of these fundamentals that I am aware of. However, I have found that, at

Features are intended to deliver a high quantity and quality of shoppers.

times, the best way to get a display is to sell a feature. For this reason, it is important to understand how to sell a feature. It has been over 30 years since Popai-Dupont published their study, and I could not find the actual graph I used, but below is a graph showing the numbers as close as I can remember. They are at least directionally correct.

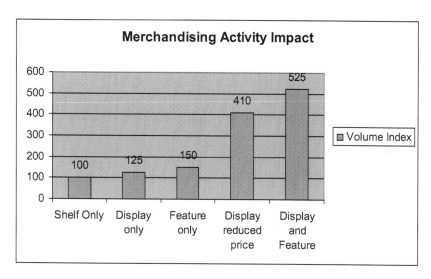

The benefit of a feature for the retailer is always connected to their shoppers. A retailer's features are intended to deliver a high quantity and quality of shoppers to their stores. This is why it is important for you to know and sell the "reach" of your products and to understand your brand's customer profile or market basket data. Let's talk "reach" first. Reach is the percent of shoppers that might use your product and thus might be interested in buying it at any time. Let's use Crest and the Dentifrice category as the example.

As you might imagine, the Dentifrice Category has a great "reach". About 90% of households use toothpaste every day and buy that category about every five weeks or so (I'm assuming the other 10% use Fixodent). This would say that most of a retailer's shoppers would be interested in a Dentifrice ad at any given point in time. Now, if you were looking for a brand to represent that category, you would want to use one of the highest share brands in the category. Crest is often the number one brand in that category and alone represents 30 to 40% of its volume. Its reach is even higher (56%) because many households have multiple brands in their house. One for mom, one for dad, and one for the kids, for example. Given this information, you would have to admit that Crest is a great candidate to represent that category in an ad. If you are suggesting multiple items for an ad idea, you can use the concept of unduplicated reach to make your story even more powerful.

Unduplicated reach is a concept that tries to estimate how many homes a group of brands might be found in. For example, Crest has a 56% reach in a category that is found in almost all homes, so you can expect to find Crest in 56% of homes all by itself. If you would add Pantene to your feature (Pantene has about 28% household reach in a category that is found in almost all homes), you could expect Pantene to be found in 28% of the 44% of homes where Crest is not found (100% - 56% = 44%), and so forth. Below is an illustration of how to calculate a multi-brand event's total unduplicated reach.

	Brand Reach	Unduplicated Reach
Crest	56.0%	56.0%
Pantene	28.0%	68.3%
Secret	30.0%	77.8%
Tide	60.0%	91.1%
Charmin	45.0%	95.1%

As you can see, with just a few of P&G's powerful brands grouped together, you can have an unduplicated reach of over 90%. This means that, not only are all of these **categories** found in virtually all homes, but you would find at least one of these **brands** in almost all homes as well.

Share and unduplicated reach address the quantity of shoppers that your suggested feature can draw into a retailer's stores, but what about the quality of those shoppers? What is a quality shopper anyway? A quality shopper is one that has the potential to spend a lot of money at your retailer's stores. That could mean that they have large families, or a high income. It could mean that they have a higher education or more discretionary income. For whatever the reason, your retailer will want to reach a lot of shoppers who are going to spend a lot of money at their stores.

There are two ways to dimensionalize the quality of the shopper your brands will bring into any retailer's stores:

-Demographic Data

-Market Basket Data

P&G and most large manufacturers have demographic data available on all of their brands. Demographic data will tell you the typical profile of the shopper who buys your brands. This will tell you if a brand appeals to a large family shopper or a high income shopper. It can also tell you if a product appeals to a particular ethnic group, as this is important for any stores with an ethnic skew in any direction. This begins to talk about the quality of the shopper your brands can bring into a store.

I think, however, the most powerful measure of the quality of a brand's shopper is its market basket data. Market basket data will tell you what else is in a shopper's basket when they buy your brand. Market Basket data can, literally, tell you when a shopper buys a brand, let's say Tide for example, on average how many dollars did that shopper spend in my store. It can also tell you exactly what else was in that shopping cart besides Tide. Of course, the idea is to appeal to a shopper that not only has a larger basket, but also a basket that is full of high profit items.

If you can show the retailer that your brands have a high reach (quantity of shoppers) and a great market basket (quality of shoppers), then you will most likely get your feature. Your buyer may, at times, be distracted by secondary motives when it comes to selecting their feature items. Motives like profit margin or absolute low cost. And while you will have to address those secondary issues in some way, it is your duty to continue to remind your buyer and your retailer that the purpose of their feature is to deliver a large quantity and a high quality of shopper to their stores, and that your brands can do the best job of doing that.

Now let's talk about display. While I don't think you should ever have a feature without a display, you can certainly have a display without a feature, and a display that also shows some value can be very nearly as effective at selling volume as a display with a feature. Now, when I say, "show a value", that does not necessarily mean a lower price, although a lower price will certainly show your shoppers a value. You can also show a value to your shoppers by offering a "special pack" at its everyday retail. A special pack can include some extra product (25% More Free) or it can include an additional item (a tube of toothpaste with a free toothbrush). You can be as creative as you like, and if you do this well, the special part of your pack becomes the incentive for your shoppers to buy. But you must remember that the purpose of a display without a feature is very different than a feature. As I stated earlier, a feature is designed to bring shoppers into a store, but a display is designed to sell more to the shoppers who are already there. The main benefits to the retailer of a display are volume and profit.

To sell a display, you need to focus on the sheer size, share and reach of a brand and category. All of these things are indicators of the likelihood of a retailer's shoppers being interested in your display when they see it in their stores. If you are going to ask a retailer to stack your brand up in their stores and encourage their shoppers to buy it, then you will probably also need to address the profit margin of your brand. This doesn't mean that you have to give it the highest margin in the category, in fact that would be a bad idea on a very competitive brand. If a retailer is making an extremely high margin on a very competitive brand, you can be assured that they will be beat on the retail price, and this can send a very negative message to a retailer's shoppers. I have found that just slightly enhancing the margin on a competitive brand can deliver the profit incentive for the retailer to display your brand while also ensuring a competitive price vs. the market.

Finally, in one way, display is very much like real estate. In real estate, there are three rules: location, location, location. While it's not the only rule in the display fundamental, location is extremely important. Most retailers have different names for their high traffic, prime display areas, but the one thing that is consistent is the high traffic. Whether it is a front

> # Display is like Real Estate.
> # The first three rules are
> # location, location, location.

endcap or action alley or front end locations, you want your display to be in one of those high traffic areas. Now, the question is, "how do you get there?"

I've found that the best way to get the best locations is to know your retailer's operations and (duh) to ask for it. The first part of this equation requires a consistent and ongoing dialogue with your retailer. You need to be constantly checking the stores to see what's going on and where the great locations are. Then you need to be asking the buyer and/or operations managers how that space is allocated. Are there programs that plan-o-gram these high traffic areas? If not, how does product get into these prime areas? Sometimes it is the sheer size of a "force out" (the amount of product that the home office forces out to the stores for an event) that dictates what brands get those locations. Sometimes it requires special secondary packaging like a display tray. Whatever the trigger, you need to know what it is, and then, don't be shy, ASK FOR IT!

The second concept that is important in the area of display has to do with the message you want to send to the shopper along with your display. Without question, the most important message that you want to include in your display is, WHAT DOES IT COST!!!! The responsibility for this part of the message really belongs more to the retailer, but there are usually things we can do to encourage this or make it easier as we design our display materials.

Outside of just price, there are other messages you can choose to send to your customers through materials that your retailer will use in their stores, like shelf cards, display trays and header cards. My counsel to you as you design these elements is to lean heavily on your marketing resources (if you have them) but do NOT abdicate the design to them. I have found that Marketing resources are great at developing the message, knowing what is important to the shoppers and how to bring that benefit out. You, however, are the in-store expert. You know what can and can't be done in the stores. Sometimes the things that can't be done are driven by your retailer's rules, and sometimes it is driven by the realities of the operation of the stores. Either way, this is what you bring to the party. Here are some simple rules that I have always used that help me contribute to the merchandising materials design process:

1. Make sure a place for price is prominent and obvious if not filled in. This will encourage your stores to make sure your display is priced. If possible, you can even put the price on it for them.
2. Keep the message simple and easy to read. You will often want to deliver multiple messages, but I would encourage you to whittle you messages down (maybe even to one) and make sure it shows up in big text. In my opinion, the smaller the text, the less likely it will be read by your shoppers.
3. Check your ideas out at store level. I would encourage you to develop some kind of prototype and take it into the store and actually put it on the display vehicle you plan it to be used on. If you are using it on an endcap, see how it looks on every shelf, not just the top one or the best one. Often, display materials look much different at the store than they do on your desk.

4. Be thrifty. You can have display materials that look great, but don't deliver the message. Don't just spend money on more colors or a nicer finish or pictures of models, unless you are convinced that they will improve the SALES of your display.

The bottom line is that if you sell consumer products, especially for P&G, you will spend much of your time selling against this Business Fundamental. The competition will be fierce because everyone wants these events that can deliver such huge chunks of incremental volume. Make sure you are clear on what YOU want and need and what the retailer wants and needs, and most importantly, ASK FOR THE ORDER! You'll never get things you don't ask for.

Introduction for Communications by Keith Johnson,

William Procter Sales master – class of 2004

Introduction:

Effective communication is the cornerstone of good selling. It is also the foundation from which we launch successful efforts to collaborate internally with P&G teammates and to build the business externally with our retail customers. This chapter brings effective communication to life with some easy to understand techniques and time tested advice that has worked for generations of successful P&G sales people.

Communications

Chapter 5

There are very few absolute requirements to being successful in sales. You can have a variety of personalities. You can have very different levels of natural intelligence and education, and of course, no race, gender or religion has a monopoly on good, successful sales people. In fact, there may only be one absolute requirement to selling, and that is the ability to communicate, and to do so persuasively. Of course, we all communicate both verbally and in writing, and I would argue that you must be good at both forms to excel in a sales career, but in this chapter I will be focusing on verbal communications.

> **Persuasive communications -**
>
> **maybe the only absolute necessity for sales success.**

It is always nice to be articulate and comfortable in your verbal communications; however, there is nothing in this, or probably any, book that will help you with that. Some people are naturally more articulate and confident in their presentation style while others become articulate and confident with practice. If you are a natural in this area, rejoice and be thankful. If you are not, just keep practicing and with time you will get there. Being glib and articulate, however, does not make you a good communicator and certainly does not make your communications persuasive, and that IS what we will be talking about in this chapter.

We will be talking about two forms of verbal communications. First we will talk about how to "present" your information in a compelling way, and then we will talk about how to gather, refine and utilize information to sell or overcome objections. Let's get started by talking about "presenting" in a persuasive fashion.

THE PERSUASIVE SELLING FORMAT

The first step in becoming a persuasive communicator is to develop knowledge of your product and your buyer. In a later chapter we will talk about the importance of having empathy for your customer or buyer. It is important to understand their wants and needs and objectives. This will definitely help you sell. You also need knowledge of the product or products that you sell. You need to know how they are made, and how well they sell and what benefits they offer to the end user, but more importantly you need to know what benefits your products deliver to your customer. Yet, even this knowledge and an articulate delivery do not guarantee you that your message will be a persuasive one. You need to take that knowledge and put it into a structure that will dramatically increase the likelihood of your success. This is where the Persuasive Selling Format comes in.

The first thing you need to do is to present your idea in a logical way that doesn't confuse the buyer AND emphasizes what the buyer will get as a result of buying! P&G found that there are five questions that a buyer needs to have answered if they are going to buy. Those five questions are:

1. What is the situation? What are the conditions that exist that cause this purchase to make sense for them?
2. What is your idea? What do you want me to do or buy?
3. How will this all work? Who has to do what and when to make this sale happen?
4. What do I get out of it? What are the benefits to me?
5. Have you made it easy for me to say, "Yes"?

Since these are the questions that buyers need to have answered, you would think that it would make sense to present your case in a format that will answer all of these questions, right! And, that is exactly what P&G did. We use what we call "The Persuasive Selling Format" to present our ideas. This is the selling format that I used 8,000 times a year in my first couple of years with the company and have used it ever since in virtually every presentation that I have given. Since they have dubbed me a "William Procter Sales Master", I guess you could say that this format is working, at least for me. Let me explain the most important aspects of each step and then we'll create some example presentations.

Summarize the Situation – This is your story. This is your set up. It will incorporate the appropriate pieces of knowledge that you have of your buyer and of your product and ties it all together with your idea. In fact, your summary of the situation or story should lead your buyer right to your idea. It can include conditions that exist for your buyer, goals that he or she has or benefits that they would like to experience. It should be compelling and personal to the buyer and lead naturally to your idea. You will see this step come to life in the examples that follow.

State Your Idea – This step needs to be clear and concise. There should be no mistake after this step about what you want your buyer to do. You say, "Who wouldn't do that?" You would be surprised how many sales are lost because the buyer doesn't know exactly what it is that the sales person wants them to buy. This is a step that won't sell your idea, but it can lose your sale if you do it poorly. We just need to make sure we don't lose the sale at this point.

Explain How it Works – This is another one of those "don't lose the sale here" steps. I can guarantee you that this is one of the things your buyer REALLY wants to know. Who does what, when and where? This step could include what exact product you want the buyer to buy. How much will it cost? When will the order need to be placed, and how much should they buy? It could even talk about exactly who should write the order and where it should be sent. It can be a very mechanical step, but it is one that needs to be covered. If it is done well, it will put the buyer's mind at ease. If done poorly, it could lead to a "no" or at least an objection of some kind.

Reinforce Key Benefits – While all of these steps are important for one reason or another, THIS one is critical. You MUST tell your buyer what he or she gets by agreeing to your idea. This will be very different depending on who your customer is and who your specific buyer is. Your idea may help your buyer reach some corporate goal in volume or profit or even inventory management. You need to know what benefit YOUR buyer is looking for. Also, it is very effective if you can allude to these benefits in your Summary of the Situation. Then, finally, you need to…

Ask for the Order (or Close) – I'm sure there are some buyers who jump across your desk half way through the presentation and demand to buy your product or idea, but you can't depend on that happening every time. In fact, it is my experience that if you don't ask for the order, you probably won't get it. This, for some people, is the most difficult part of the presentation. This is where your idea will either be accepted or rejected. "REJECTED?" you say. I just don't think I can handle the rejection. Well, McFly, if you don't ask for the order, your chance for rejection goes way up, so you might as well increase your chances of acceptance by closing! There are many techniques for Asking for The Order, but just to get you started, I'll share with you my three personal favorites:

1**. The Assumptive Close** – "I'll go get the paperwork and we can start writing up your order." This technique doesn't ask for the order, it assumes the buyer is going to order and the sales person just moves to what would be the next step, which is writing up the order.

2. **The Choice Close** - "Would you like to run the feature and display in November or December?" This technique offers the buyer choices, both of which are good for you AND agrees to the purchase.

3. **Minor to Major** - Propose a series of easy to make, minor decisions that together add up to a major one.

It has even been argued that if there is such a thing as a one step selling presentation, it consists of the "Close" step. If you have ever had a girl scout at your door, you have probably seen a one step presentation, "Would you like to by some of my cookies?" Even if you say yes, you will probably find yourself covering the other steps as you complete your order. You will probably ask how much they cost, and when you are going to get them and how. You might even talk about which cookies tastes the best or which ones are healthier (who are you kidding?). So, at P&G, instead

> # If you don't ask
> # for the order,
> # you probably won't
> # get it!!

of just asking for the order, we go through the formality of walking our buyers through the other steps. Or it could be that at P&G we are asking for bigger orders than just a box of cookies, and the Persuasive Selling Format enhances the chance of a successful conclusion.

OK, let's put some of this "format" theory into practice. Just to prove how effective the Persuasive Selling Format is, I'll walk us through one of my favorite training exercises for the PSF. We are going to create a presentation to sell my wife on going camping. Now, to set the stage, my wife's idea of roughing it is to go to the Holiday Inn instead of the Hyatt. I always pretend during this exercise that we still have young children, just to add a little challenge to the sale. I've used this exercise with at least a dozen groups, and the presentations always come out a little like the example below.

Summary of the Situation:
    -Our life is stressful
        -Kids, work, cell phones. We just can't get away.
    -Wouldn't it be great to get away from it all just for a while.
    -A great way to REALLY get away is camping.
        -Fresh air, leave our cell phones behind, no distractions.
        -Northwest Arkansas is the camping capital of the US.

State the Idea:
    -We need to take advantage and go camping this weekend.

Explain How it Works:
    -I have already arranged for the neighbor to watch the kids.
    -I found two camp grounds that offer first class cabins – no tents.
    -Notice I'm setting up my Choice close.
    -I've already bought the supplies and will do all the cooking!
    -Both camp grounds offer your favorite activities, tennis and horse back riding.

Reinforce Key Benefits:
    -We will get away from the hustle and bustle of work, kids, etc.
    -We'll get out in the healthy, fresh air.
    -We can have some private, intimate time together.
    -We'll have a blast playing tennis and horseback riding.
    -We'll come back rested and refreshed to tackle the world again.

Close (Easy Next Step):
    -Now, do you want to camp at Devils Den or Beaver Lake?

I have found that this exercise helps people grasp the structure and intent of the Persuasive Selling Format. Trust me, however, that it works very effectively in business also. I have used it constantly for the last 30+ years. On pages 48 through 50 is an example of a presentation that I actually delivered to Walmart. I've taken out any confidential information, but I think you can get the idea of how this format can work in all kinds of selling situations. Notice that it starts with my favorite "lead in" slide, and it flows perfectly with the Persuasive Selling Format.

My last counsel would be to use this format every chance you get. I was lucky enough to be hired during a time that forced me to practice this format 8,000 times a year. While you may not be able to do that, you should use it in every selling situation with which you are confronted. The goal is to make the format and the thought process second nature.

HANDLING OBJECTIONS

No matter how skilled you are, or become, as a salesperson, you will always be confronted by, and have to deal with, objections. Hopefully, if you are REALLY good and have done a good job of understanding your buyer, you will be able to avoid some objections by anticipating them and building answers to them into your presentations. However, even the most skilled sales people cannot anticipate every objection, so in order to be effective and persuasive you will need to understand the secret to handling objections.

Now, instinctively you may think that the secret to overcoming objections is just selling. That makes sense, right? If someone objects to something in your presentation, you just need to sell them harder. This actually is a temptation that some very good salespeople need to overcome, because when someone says "no" to your proposal or objects to something during your presentation, what you really need is INFORMATION. You need to determine what exactly are they objecting to, and why. Instead of selling, which is a natural reaction for most of us, you need to start asking questions or using other techniques that will give you more information. The information that you gather will help you to overcome the objection.

Working together to deliver Superior Results !

Toothbrushes and Toothpaste
The Marriage Made in Heaven

- Leverage Toothpaste planned purchases to sell Manual Toothbrushes:
    - **Toothpaste** is a planned purchase in **49%** of all Oral Care shopping trips.
    - **Toothbrushes** are only planned **12%** of the time.
    - Currently, shoppers only buy brushes about every six months despite the fact that dentists recommend changing every three months!
- Manual Toothbrushes help sweeten the Oral Care market basket profit mix!
    - Toothpaste category ave. margin is XX% (est.)
    - Manual Toothbrush margin is XX% (P&G current qtr.)
- Wal*Mart data shows dramatic increase in MTB sales when merchandised with Toothpaste.
    - Our Feb 03 event delivered a 122 index on toothbrushes over three weeks (a 137 index in the first week!).
    - That was $X.X million in sales ($XXX,XXX incremental) and $XXX,XXX in profit ($XX,XXX incremental) for that three week display period.
    - This was (by far) the best MTB performance of the year. Even bigger than Christmas!!

Crest!

- Display Crest In March Using a Toothpaste – Toothbrush Regimen PDQ.

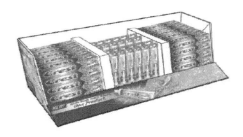

The Details

- PDQ will be packed as the items sell at Wal*Mart !!
  - X.X weeks business of both Toothbrushes and Toothpaste for full 4 – Way Display.
  - This is fewer weeks inventory than a Toothpaste only 4 – Way.
- Will write Store Specific Orders in January for your review.

Oral Care Regimen Sales

- Your Shoppers obviously like it.
  - They have shown this in the past by voting with their dollars (purchases).
- Your Associates like it.
  - They love the labor savings of our PDQ's
  - And since they are custom PDQ's for WM only, we pack them as they sell at WM.
- Even YOU have to like the **incremental dollar volume and Profit** and **reduced inventory!**
- So, What's wrong with this picture. **If Sam were here, he'd say:**

The real key to overcoming objections is gathering and refining information. P&G teaches a series of communications techniques and two models that, arguably, do the same thing or, at a minimum, are inter-related. Let's first talk about the communications techniques that P&G

> **The key to overcoming objections is gathering and refining information.**

taught me over 30 years ago to overcome an objection. Below is a list of techniques that you can use when the buyer objects, or, as P&G puts it, when the buyer's "shade is down". This means that the buyer is not cooperative, and you want to "open up the shade", or get some cooperation. You should notice a certain progression in these techniques, and that is intentional. Here they are:

-General Leads

> -These are not so much questions as techniques that will get the buyer to continue to talk and give you more information. A General Lead may sound like, "Tell me more about that" or simply saying "go on".

-Restatements

> -This is exactly what it sounds like. It is restating what the buyer says with a question mark at the end of it. The buyer, for example, makes the statement, "We only display that item at the front end." Then you say, "You only display it at the front end?" This is like saying, "why is that", and hopefully you will get an explanation – more information.

-Pauses

> -This is where you are silent after a buyer's statement and hopefully the buyer will fill the silence with further

information. Be careful with this technique. Give it some time to work, but not so much that the situation gets uncomfortable. Remember, this is not a contest to see who will talk first. The whole idea is to get more information. If the pause doesn't work, move on to another technique.

-Comfortable Probes

-A probe is simply a question. "How does your modular process work?" This is not usually a very sensitive question and the answer will probably result in a wealth of information.

-Sensitive Probes

-This is just another kind of question, but aimed at more sensitive information. "What would your boss think of this idea?" or "How would this impact your compensation?" Or "What happened when..." This is the kind of question that you can only ask once the buyer has shown some signs of cooperation. This is a fairly aggressive technique and you need to be careful with your timing, but questions like this can yield a tremendous depth of information for you to use.

-Interpretations

-You could argue that this is the most aggressive of the communication techniques, even more aggressive than a sensitive probe, because it adds to or subtly changes the direction of what your buyer has said based on your "read" of the information received. An interpretation usually starts out something like this, "What you are telling me is..." or "So, if I have heard you correctly..."

Early on, when the buyer is not cooperating or you don't really know what the problem is, you will notice that the techniques are less aggressive and designed to get you information. This information will usually help you identify the real issues, especially if you use the proper techniques along the way. The more information you get, the more open the buyer becomes (because he or she is giving you that information) and the more likely it is that you will find the true objection, issue, or problem. The deeper you get into the process, the more aggressive you can get with your communications techniques. This is the PROGRESSION that I was talking about earlier.

P&G also teaches an objection handling process called D.U.V.H. (pronounced Dove) that actually does the same thing. D.U.V.H. stands for:

-Determine

-Understand

-Verify, and

-Handle

This process starts with an objection, and, believe it or not, buyers will sometimes not explain their objection or (heaven forbid) they may even give you a false or misleading objection in the beginning. In the **Determine** stage you are gathering information to figure out what the real problem is, and in this stage you will use the less aggressive techniques like general leads and restatements. As the buyer pours out the information, you will start getting an idea of what the real issues are. At that point you need to start to **Understand** the situation. In this stage you will be able to use the more aggressive techniques, like comfortable or even sensitive probes, to help you focus in on the real problems. Finally, in the **Verify** stage, you will use the most aggressive techniques like sensitive probes or interpretations to confirm EXACTLY what is getting in the way. When you can say, "So, the real issue is _____." Or "So, if I can fix _____, then we can get together." Then you are out of the clarification process and you can **Handle** the objection, issue or problem. At this point you are selling again.

Recently, we have started teaching a process called Persuasive Questioning. This is a selling process that allows the buyer to sell him or herself, which can be very powerful. If you have ever seen anyone pursue an idea that they thought was their own, you know what I mean. However, to be absolutely honest, Persuasive Questioning is the same thing as using the Communication Skills or the D.U.V.H. model above. Of course, it has its own "new" steps which are made up of the four "I" questions; **Information, Issues, Impact and Importance.** The reality is, however, this is just an objection handling process that ASSUMES the objection from the very beginning.

In the **information** stage, you would use the less aggressive techniques like general leads and restatements to gather information. Let's say that you want to sell your buyer on a new item, you assume the buyer has objected and you start with a question like, "Tell me about your new item implementation process." This is just a general lead and will get you a mountain of information, including (probably) what they require of new items. If you don't get that directly, you can use another technique to get you there. Next, you want to identify the **Issues** that your buyer encounters in this process so that you can make sure that your idea either answers those issues or avoids them. In this stage, you are probably using a little more aggressive techniques like restatements, pauses and comfortable probes. As you try to identify the **Impact** of the key issue or issues, you will probably be using even more aggressive techniques like sensitive probes. Finally, in the **Importance** stage, you are doing the same thing that you would do in the Verify stage in the D.U.V.H. process, and you are probably using similar techniques like interpretations or sensitive probes. A satisfactory conclusion to a Persuasive Questioning session might sound something like this, "So, if I've heard you correctly, for my new items to get into the modular quickly, we will need to..."

It's not the Process, It's the Sale!

The important thing to remember is what you are trying to accomplish. You are trying to overcome an objection and make a sale. You don't get extra points from your buyer for using all of the "I" questions in your presentation, or going through all of the steps of the D.U.V.H. model. You ARE successful if you walk out with the order that you wanted.

What you DO need to do when you get an objection (or assume one as in the PQ model) is to stop selling, start gathering information, and start listening so that you can refine that information and identify and eventually handle the real issues. It makes sense to use the less aggressive techniques to gather the information, to get the buyer talking and to raise his or her shade. As the shade goes up and as you have gathered more information to use, you can and should use more aggressive techniques to help you narrow in on your target. And once you have identified your target, you can sell again, hopefully and instinctively using the Persuasive Selling Format. It has worked for me for over 30 years, and it will work for you if you have the discipline to use it every day in every aspect of your life.

It reminds me of the story of the tourist who stopped a musician in New York and asked him, "How do I get to Carnegie Hall?" To which the musician answered, "Practice, Practice, Practice!" It is the same with becoming a persuasive communicator. You need to Practice, Practice, Practice!

Introduction for Shelf Management by Jim Cannan,

William Procter Sales master – class of 2004

Introduction:

Reading Kevin's chapter on shelf management reminded me of the huge influence retail sales reps had on product presentation to shoppers back in the old days. The shelf was like your report card and it was often very evident that some people had a real passion and talent for shelf arrangement, and some didn't. Not surprisingly, our reps with the best looking shelves were always at the top in terms of reaching sales quota. Shelf is probably even more important today given SKU proliferation and the fragmented media environment. Showcasing leading brands with prime space and position is an absolute "must" if those brands are going to reach their full sales potential. Providing our retail partners with data based shelving recommendations is more important today than ever before.

Shelf Management

Chapter 6

In 1974, Richard Nixon was President, Bill Gates was a sophomore at Harvard, P & G sold $6 billion in sales and I began my career in Procter & Gamble's Sales Department in the Toilet Goods Division. As you might imagine, things were a little different in the market place. Walmart was a sleepy 110 store chain mostly in Missouri and Arkansas, Walgreen's had just over 600 stores and Woolworth's 300 Woolco stores were still a bit of the rage. The consolidation in the trade, which you are living with today, had not even occurred yet. The trade was much more fragmented than it is today, and some very important decisions were still made at store level.

Back then, we shipped directly to about 5,000 customers in the United States vs. the 500 customers we ship to today (2006). As you might imagine, our sales people could have tremendous influence on the business fundamentals (Distribution, Shelving, Pricing and Merchandising) for each of these direct buying accounts. Even the big chains like Kroger, Albertson's and K-Mart allowed tremendous flexibility at store level to make decisions. Stores could decide not to carry items that were authorized for them, they could buy displays on their own and they could even make changes (sometimes radical) on their shelf plan-o-grams if they so desired. Of course, P&G needed to have a sales force that could operate effectively in that environment.

In order to cover these thousands of direct selling accounts and to call on and influence virtually every chain store we needed an army of full time professional sales people. Enter Kevin Canfield from Ball State University in Indiana and hundreds more just like me. And, for about every four of me, there needed to be a Unit Manager and for about every four Unit Managers, there needed to be a District Manager and so on. Of course, since we had four other Sales Divisions, each one had to have their own sales force to do the same thing for them. You do the math; we had a ton of people out on the streets selling our products. The ongoing joke was that there could be a five car wreck in the Kroger parking lot and all five cars could be driven by P & G sales reps.

In some ways, it was the best of times, and in some ways the worst. Those days offered a great training environment. Unit Managers spent a tremendous amount of time with their sales reps, especially in the first few months of their training. Also, the work itself gave us all great sales experience. In the average day, for example, we were expected to call on 11 stores and to try to sell at least three "things" per call. When I say "thing", that could be a display, a new item into distribution or a shelf change. I did the math for you in an earlier chapter. That was about 8,000 selling situations per year.

Now, the King of "things" to sell back then was a display. That was the thing that we put most of our emphasis on. In fact, we also measured and put significant emphasis on "personally erected" displays. A real home run was to sell a display where the product would be delivered to the store on the day of your next call so that you could come in and build the display yourself. It was as if a display built by our sales reps had more value or sold product better than displays built by the stores' people. In fact, I remember being disappointed if the product came in early and the store people put the display up for me. They would be so proud of themselves and I would be sort of "bummed", although I would never let them know. The reality was that we emphasized "personally erected" displays because we were convinced as a company that it would increase our total displays, which was the key measure of success. The intention was good, but I'm sure it drove some bad behavior.

So, you're saying, I thought this chapter was supposed to be on Shelf Management? Where did that come into play back then? The reality is that "shelf improvements" was a barely measured statistic in those days. There was a column on our daily report (which was a hard copy pad that hung from our car's steering wheel which we filled out in triplicate) where a sales rep could take credit for a shelf improvement; however, I don't ever remember any award for the person with the most shelf improvements.

By this slight, I'm sure that the company was NOT saying that shelf improvements were not important, but rather that it was just too difficult to measure. What was a shelf improvement? What was its value? How do you compare one shelf change to another? In the area of display, it was a little easier to measure. First, it had to exist! It had to be in a secondary location and it had to be at least five cases of product or more. Second, size was everything. A 50 case display was better than a 10 case display, maybe even five times better.

In this environment, where display was king and shelf was a distant second choice, I developed a real interest in the shelf. It had to be instincts, because I didn't know some of the facts about the shelf back then that I do today. For example:

-Depending on the category, 80-95% of our volume is sold off the shelf.

-At Walmart 80% of their inventory is on their shelves in their stores, and

-In 2007, Walmart finished the year with almost $34 billion in inventory, their #1 investment.

I didn't know any of this, but for some reason I became a bit of a fanatic about the shelf. I made it a rule to ask for at least one shelf improvement in every call I made, and these could be very time consuming, taking away time that I could spend on the king of measurements, display. Even a small change, like increasing the number of facings for one of our brands, could take 15 to 30 minutes since it usually required reducing facings of other brands and possibly handling some excess inventory. Complete department resets where I would change the locations of our brands on the shelves could take hours, even with help.

There was another reason why my focus on the shelf didn't make any sense. It was hard! Most store managers or department heads were used to buying or turning down display ideas. Most were not very interested in changing their shelf. Their usual comeback was, "this is what the Headquarters recommends, why should I change it?" This is when I began to realize the benefits of fixing a problem on the shelf, and I made sure I always included one or more of those benefits in each presentation. For example, low inventory or an out-of-stock was a

> # The shelf is more than a storage unit, it is a selling tool as well!!

sign of an item or brand that needed more space and excessive inventory was a sign of an item that had too much space. Sometimes I actually increased my empty space and took product in the back room of an item that I had to reduce to get it. In the short term that might not have been the best thing to do, but in the long run, it was!

Even back then I knew that the shelf was more than a storage unit; it was a selling tool as well. Consequently there was always a little bit of art and a little bit of science to each shelf change that I sold. Back then and today, I focused on the same benefits to the retailer:

-**Increased Sales**
- -Sometimes by reducing out of stocks.
  - -By moving bigger brands to the best shelves (usually eye level), and
- -Moving smaller brands down.
  - -The net effect of these last two moves is a positive for the retailer.
  - -Because the Department is easier to shop. This is clearly an "art" factor.

-**Reduced Costs**
- -Reduce or eliminate unproductive inventory
- -Making the Department easier to stock.
- -Reduced complexity.

-**Satisfy the Shopper**
- -Always have what they want to buy. This covers distribution and in-stock.
- -Make the shoppers' brands easier to find and thus to buy.

After a couple of years of retail coverage, I was finally moved to DFR (a District Field Representative), and then finally to Unit Manager. These positions offered me my first taste of selling the big chain accounts. For the first few years I focused on the same things all the Unit Managers were focused on, and that was selling my accounts on advertising our brands in the newspapers, and then hopefully displaying those brands at store level to support those ads. We had new items and brands to launch and special initiatives, of course, but I spent most of my time selling features and displays, and I was pretty good at it too. I delivered my quota every year and I thought I had the game pretty well figured out. I had pretty much forgotten about the shelf.

Then, one day I was working with one of my sales reps and we were calling on a Shop'N'Save store in Pittsburgh, PA. Shop'N'Save was a chain of about 150 stores that was supplied by a wholesaler name Charley

Brothers, which was my largest account. The Charley Brothers actually owned about half of the stores and franchised the rest of the stores to individuals who tied into all of Shop'N'Save's features and advertising campaigns. For all intents and purposes, it was a chain.

We had done our store check, built a display and sold another with a hand carried survey, and we felt pretty good about ourselves. We were about to leave when I challenged the sales rep to fix the Shampoo and Conditioner Department. We had just launched Pert, and the shelf space was obviously not sufficient in this store because we were out of a couple of items. I reverted back to my old sales rep days and helped my sales rep construct a solid sales presentation full of benefits. Now, this store was a franchise store so the person we were going to talk to actually owned the store and these benefits were even more meaningful to him. So we hit him with a solid 1-2-3 punch:

Increased Sales
Improved In-stock
Satisfied Shoppers

We were asking for a big change. We wanted to move Pert up and give it more space, which meant moving some other brands down and giving them less space. In addition to the benefits I outlined above I told my Sales Rep about my magic close I used when I was in the field, and we used it! We told him we were going to increase his sales, make his department look better, BUT if he didn't like the changes that we made when we were finished, we would change it right back. Now, I'm not sure how magic that close is, but in the two years I worked in the field, I NEVER had anyone ask me to change it back! And we didn't have to change it back that day in Pittsburgh either!

When we were done, I stepped back to admire our handiwork. Wow! That Department looked great and I said to myself, "I wish every Shop 'N' Save store looked like this!" Then, I thought to myself, why not? Maybe I could sell my buyer on creating a plan-o-gram like this and sending it out to all their stores. Now, that would be a big sale, I thought. I wasn't sure how big, but I had to believe it would be big.

So, that's what I decided to do. I planned my presentation to look a lot like the presentations I used to give in the field, and of course in the field I would always show the store managers examples of the flaws I saw in his or her current shelf layout. In order to replicate this, I had my Sales Reps canvass 30 of the Shop 'N' Save stores and gather some data. I had them tell me how the recent new items, like Pert, were being handled and how many out of stocks they found in the Shampoo and Conditioner section. I threw in a new concept called "consistency" and on the next page you will see how the presentation eventually went:

> Summary of the Situation:
>> -We have done a survey of 30 of your stores, and here is what we found.
>> - Your Shampoo & Conditioner plan-o-grams were very inconsistent.
>> - 20% of your stores do not have Pert on the shelf yet.
>> -Your stores are running about a 10% out of stock rate in that Department.
>> -Your shoppers have too many other options (other retailers) to allow this trend to continue.
>
> State the Idea:
>> -You need a plan-o-gram that manages your space more efficiently and is consistent across all of your stores to better satisfy your shoppers.
>
> How it Works:
>> -Here is a sample modular that:
>>> -Invests your space according to sales.
>>>> -Features the top brands to maximize sales, and
>>>> -Emphasizes new items to take advantage of introductory efforts.
>>> -Then I took his input and built that into the plan-o-gram.
>>> -My Sales Reps can help your Department Heads implement the plan-o-gram within a month of release.

Benefits:

> -Just reducing Out of Stocks to 5% would increase sales by over $150,000 per year for the chain. (Back then, this was BIG money)
>
> -Your stores would better implement all new items, which could lead to over $300,000 per year per introduction (using Pert as the average).
>
> -You would better meet your shopper's needs in terms of in-stock and ease of shopping and consistency throughout the chain.

Close:

> The sooner we get this out, the sooner you reap the benefits. I'll write a note from you to the stores explaining what we are doing, you can send it out to the stores next week and my Sales Reps can be in the stores the following week helping them with the change!

Now, that was about 27 years ago, so that may not be EXACTLY how it went, but it's pretty close. I included this presentation for a couple of reasons. First, most of you are probably saying, "That's no big deal. I could do that." And, you're right. I've sold everyone from Kroger store managers to the Walmart's Headquarters, and I have found that simple, logical ideas that focus on their benefits usually work. Second, I would always encourage you to get buyer input and build it into your idea. You can see that in the "How it Works" section above. This is the Headquarters version of the magic close. Once you work their ideas into your concept, it becomes theirs, and who likes to say no to their own ideas?

> **Display is nice, but shelf is RELENTLESS !!**

Now, you have to remember that this was back in the early 80's and we did many things very differently back then. We had just gotten rid of the stone and chisel for recording history and had developed the ball point pen and lined paper. This might be a little bit of an exaggeration, but times were different. For example, every two weeks I took a physical inventory at Charley Bro. and calculated the movement on each of our items in order to forecast how much they needed to order for the warehouse. After I did this 100 times or so, I became VERY familiar with the pattern of sales for all of your brands. When our new modular hit the stores, the impact on sales was immediate and almost unbelievable. Virtually every item increased in sales, and in many cases they had increased as much as 50%. As I wrote my bi-weekly orders, I could FEEL the business impact of the changes we had made. And, the real beauty of this was that this increase didn't stop after a week or so like a display's impact. It continued on for the rest of the year. This experience changed my approach to selling our business. It is when I first discovered that, while displays are nice, the **Shelf is Relentless**. It can be selling our brands (or not) 24-7-365.

This simple presentation eventually led to a modular plan-o-gram process where I was the captain (for lack of a better word) for all of our categories. Both Charley Bros and my businesses thrived over the next few years. My business at Charley Bros. indexed in the mid to high 120's over the next two years until the initial volume increase was built into our base, and my unit shipped quota for the next four years in a row.

Most importantly, our brands developed a share premium vs. the U.S. almost immediately and continued until after I stopped calling on Charley Bro. I was a shelf "believer" and would continue to be one for the rest of my career.

After Pittsburgh, I went to Cincinnati on a Special Assignment and ran our Sales Schools for new Sales Reps and new Unit Managers. I eventually went to San Francisco as a District Manager, where I spent most of my time working with my Unit Managers and Sales Reps. I, hopefully, transferred some of my selling experience to them, but for the most part, this old role took me away from the direct selling role that I was pretty good at.

In the early 90's, we began to restructure our sales force. This restructure focused on two things that impacted me directly. First, we started to organize around our customers rather that around geographies. By now, I think we would all say that was a good idea. Second, we started putting our District Managers (hopefully some of our best sales people) back up against our biggest customers. How did this impact me? It wasn't long after this that I was on a plane to Fayetteville, Arkansas to call on Walmart to manage what was then our "Beauty Care" business.

Before I move on, I feel I have to make a little disclaimer here. At the time that I moved to the Walmart Team, I think the company was having trouble getting people to go to Fayetteville. I was born in a small town in Indiana, and Fayetteville actually reminded me a little of home. In fact, I've always said that Fayetteville was like, "Indiana with an accent." Today, the team is much bigger and even higher profile, and Northwest Arkansas has developed tremendously. It's a great place to spend all or part of your career, but 14 years ago I was one of a few that actually wanted to go there.

When I first took over the Beauty Care business at Walmart, we had plenty of opportunities. By necessity, I was drawn into the feature and display rat race, but we put together a long term plan, which allowed me to sell six months worth of merchandising at a time. This gave me the time to get involved with their Modular Planning Process, Walmart's version of plan-o-grams.

The first buyer that I dealt with in Hair Care was Kirk Hessington. He was a pretty prototypical buyer in that he bled Walmart blue. His "yes" meant "yes" and his "no" meant "no", and his word or his hand shake was as good as a signed contract. Kirk certainly didn't buy everything I tried to sell him, but for the reasons mentioned above, he was a pleasure to deal with. Also, he had a plan on how he wanted to grow the category's business, but he had an open mind for things that would work better. His bottom line was the top line. If you gave him ideas that built his business, that sold his shoppers more Hair Care, he was interested. I LOVE buyers like Kirk!

Back in 1992, Walmart's Hair Care modular philosophy was a little bit of a hodge-podge. Some brands ran horizontally, and some were blocked. Their major focus was to carry the right items and to give them the right amount of space. Now that is not a bad approach. It is just a little one dimensional. As I said earlier, the shelf is both a storage unit and a selling tool. This approach was much more focused on the storage unit role of the shelf. After I stared at their set long enough in their layout room, I began to get an idea that would be good for me and good for Walmart, and that idea revolved around the other aspects of the shelf, the shelf as a selling tool.

At this point, I want to emphasize that while Walmart was huge back in '92 and it is the largest customer in the world today, the techniques I used and the concepts that I sold were not much different than the ones I sold to Kroger managers back in 1974. I would like to think that my ideas were on the leading edge of thinking at the time and were particularly well aimed at this Customer and this buyer, but they were simple and time tested. I won't walk you through the entire presentation, but here are the basic concepts.

> 1.) We would block the brands using their four foot sections as natural boundaries for our blocks, which would:
>   -Allow many more brands to participate in the eye level shelf,
>   -Make all brands easier to find by the shoppers.
>   -Make it easier for their Associates to implement and maintain the modular.
> 2.) We would actually use the colors of the brands' bottles to create "frames" for each other. Imagine a white colored brand bottle next to a dark color (say red) bottle next to another white bottle, next to another dark color (say blue). Below is a simulation of what that would look like. This would:
>   -Make each brand "POP".
>   -Again, make it easier for the shopper to find her brand.
>   -This was good for ALL brands, not just mine.

3.) We would arrange the brands by price point from left to right. This would:

-Encourage shoppers to trade up to higher dollar ring brands.

-Again, make it easier for the shopper to find HER brand.

We, of course, applied the usual good "storage unit" decisions to these concepts and created a modular (plan-o-gram) that really worked. For

> # The shelf is the foundation for the other Business Fundamentals

confidentiality reasons, I can't share the exact results, but I can say that for the next four years, Walmart grew its share of the Shampoo and Conditioner business significantly faster than they grew their total business, which, back then was +10% comps and +15-20% in total.

During this period, my business thrived also. We tripled the size of our Beauty Care business in just four years, and I won four Gold Awards and one Chairman's Club award, over those four years. During these years, I was even further convinced of the importance of shelf to the business. I found that it was the true foundation of my business. Merchandising was easier to sell because shoppers were voting for my brands with their dollar purchases everyday, and the shelf more easily absorbed the aftermath of all the displays that I sold. New items were easier to sell in because my buyers "believed" in my existing brands, which created an environment of positive expectations for anything new that I was presenting. The shelf was the foundation on which I developed my other business fundamentals!

After a short stint in the Food/Beverage division managing our Pringles, Crisco, and Jif businesses at both Sam's and Walmart, I was asked to come over to manage our Oral Care Business at Walmart. This was a critical time for Oral Care at Walmart in the US. Crest had fallen to the number two ranked toothpaste brand significantly behind Colgate, and we were about to launch a new tooth whitening product under the Crest name, Crest Whitestrips. While the launch of Crest Whitestrips was VERY important to me and to the company, Crest toothpaste was still Oral Care's largest brand, one of the company jewels and my biggest opportunity. I needed to get that ship turned around.

The good news was that I had another great buyer, Joe Grady. He was very much like Kirk Hessington in many ways. His "yes" meant "yes" and his "no" meant "no", and he was very willing to take risks to build the business and to take responsibility for his actions. If he was convinced that an idea could deliver the top line volume that he was looking for, he was willing to try just about anything. By this time, the AE's (me) were not working in the layout room anymore. We had Shelf Analysts to do that work, but while the Analyst did the work, we worked as a team on the concepts that we felt could drive the business for Walmart and for P&G. The concept our team developed was called the "T Bone" modular.

As usual, the concepts we used in this set were not earthshaking, but they made sense for THIS category, for THIS customer at THIS time. We wanted to create a modular that would:

-Drive the Top two brands in the category, Crest and Colgate, but not at the expense of each other.
-Use these top two brands to drive the entire Dentifrice Category and even drive all of Oral Care.
-Feature the newly launched Whitening Kit Category.
-Encourage Sales of the very profitable Toothbrush Category every time one of their customers bought Toothpaste. The Toothbrush Category also had tremendous potential for increased sales if we could just get people to replace their brushes as often as dentists suggested.

We accomplished all of this by, first, putting Crest and Colgate in featured positions but on opposite sides of the modular. Next, we featured the new Whitening Kit category right in the middle of the high volume, high in-home penetration Dentifrice Category and, finally, we encouraged Toothbrush sales by running that category along the top of the Dentifrice Category. When you put all of these ideas together, they were designed to increase volume and profit of the entire Oral Care Category. Now, what's wrong with that picture – NOTHING!

> **Watching your shoppers shop can teach you much about how to help them buy.**

This concept worked for Walmart for the next five years and delivered everything (maybe even a little more) that we promised. Walmart captured a disproportionately high share of the new Whitestrips Category and they did the same with the Toothbrush and Toothpaste categories. Consequently, they grew their share of total Oral Care significantly faster than they built total store volume. All of that was a sign that the set was working.

From a personal perspective, we grew Crest's share of Dentifrice at Walmart significantly faster than the rest of the U.S. All of Oral Care grew at Walmart, and we were even able to build our profitability, which we will talk about in later chapters. Finally, at the end of my tenure in Oral Care on the Walmart Team, I was named one of the original four William Procter Sales Master in North America for the Company. I'm pretty sure there was a connection.

Certainly, I did more in the four plus years in Oral Care than just develop this modular concept, but this modular created the foundation for my business. My merchandising flourished. My new item launches were extremely successful, partially because Walmart was very focused on winning with new items, but also because the health of my business made them EXPECT success from our new items. The "T Bone" set was a stable platform from which to operate.

There are several morals of this shelf story, and I hope these have all become evident in this chapter:

1. Think from the Customer's (the retailer's) perspective!
2. Know their goals and objectives and their really "won't do's".
3. Find and focus on your customer's benefits, and make sure you -
4. Deliver what you promise.
5. Finally, and this may not have come out earlier, deliver on the little things. Deliver on the day to day paper work that can make their (the buyer and buyer's assistant) lives easier.

It doesn't take a rocket scientist to do the sales job with excellence! In an earlier chapter I suggested that 90% of success is just showing up! I don't know if it's 90%, but just showing up, everyday, with your best effort is a big part of being successful. Believing in yourself and looking from the Customer's perspective will add real quality to your presence. If you want to become a master at sales, you can. Just believe, and just do it!

Finally, you should be having some fun. A wise man once told me that, "things are never as bad as you think or as good as you think." Keep yourself balanced. Don't get too down on yourself or become too euphoric. Keep an even keel and enjoy the ride.

Introduction for Empathy by Tim Linehan,

William Procter Sales master – class of 2006

Introduction:

When I started with P&G 25 years ago, my first real boss, Ernie Addy (Philadelphia Food Sales District Manager) told me on the first day on the job that I had two things that I needed to do. First, I had to sell the company's brands and then, second, I had to help the customer re-sell them.

For me to do that, he said that I needed to possess three things;

1-Knowledge of the strengths and benefits of our brands.

2-Selling skills, and finally

3-Empathy for our customers.

In my opinion, none of these three things have changed!

Empathy

Chapter 7

When I started with the company in 1974, I instinctively possessed a quality that helped me sell my customers. I had empathy for them. Notice, I didn't say that I had sympathy for my customers. I had empathy for them. I tried to see things from their point of view. I tried to understand their situation. This helped me to identify the benefits that my products could deliver specifically to them. This made my ideas much more persuasive and acceptable to my customers. I always thought that this quality in me was important, but I never said much about it to anyone else. 31 years later, the company validated my feelings.

In 2005 we executed the largest survey within P&G that I am aware of, to determine which skills were most important for people to possess if they were going to be successful in our kind of sales. We interviewed over 100 people including P&G managers and the William Procter Sales Masters as well as Customer buyers and managers. Through these interviews we identified four basic competency areas and 17 skills that fall under those competencies.

During these interviews, we also asked our participants which of these competencies and skills were the most important. Lo and behold, the interviewees indicated that Selling and Relationship Management was the most important competency and Understanding Customer Needs was the most important skill. This sounds a lot like empathy to me. In fact, if you look up the word "empathy" in Webster's Dictionary, you will find this definition:

> Empathy - action of understanding, being aware of, being sensitive to, and vicariously experiencing the feelings, thoughts, and experience of another…

If you have this skill, you should use it, and even rely on it. People without this skill may even try to dissuade you. Their arguments will usually revolve around doing what is right for you at the expense of the customer. Resist! Your instincts will guide you and in the long run, if you continue to do what is right for your customer, YOU will win also.

If you don't have this skill, you can develop it or at least simulate it through knowledge of your customer. If you really study your customer you will at least be aware of their needs, their objectives and their strategies even if you don't become sensitive to them. In that case you will have accomplished at least half of the definition of empathy. With a little luck and a lot of study, you may even become empathetic to your customer,

It's Empathy not sympathy that's needed!

and the effectiveness of your selling presentations will go WAY up. By the way, if you already have this skill, a little study of your customer will only serve to strengthen it. So, here are a few things that you should do to build, simulate and/or stimulate the empathetic skill:

1. Subscribe to a trade journal or two. Whether you get them in the mail or electronically, they will keep you up to date with the latest (obvious) news on your customer and their channel and their competition. If you don't know this information, you will eventually be embarrassed by your lack of knowledge of the customer. Some of my favorites are:
   a. Discount Store News (remember, I called on Walmart)
   b. The Wall Street Journal (I get this online)
   c. Chain Drug News
   d. Food Store News

   These will keep you knowledgeable of your customer and all of the major channels of trade with which they compete.
2. Create a portfolio in Yahoo Finance. In that portfolio, I would list my account, of course, and all of the major competitors that they are concerned about. This will give you daily and even hourly updates on articles that mention these customers. I would recommend that you put a few of your competitors in that portfolio also. I track Colgate, Unilever, and Kimberly Clark ,just to mention the obvious few.
3. Get your hands on your customer's annual report. If your customer is publicly held, you can do this by simply buying a share of stock in that company. This should entitle you to a copy of their annual report when it comes out. If this is not possible, most companies have a copy of their annual report on their website. These annual reports will give you the numbers that you should be familiar with, and they will also give you the broad strategies that your customer is employing as well as the subtle messages of how they are progressing vs. their objectives.

> **Without empathy, you are just another selfish voice to the Customer.**

4. Ask your customer. You need to find time to ask your buyer and his or her boss some questions. How are things going? What are your most important objectives? What is hot corporately? What can I do to help? You may be surprised at

the answers. After you've asked the questions, go into the stores and see if there is any evidence of the answers you just heard or if you see other issues. What is the stores' in-stock position? Are they clean? Are they over-stocked? With what? What are the themes that you see in the stores? All of this will help you get a handle on what they are trying to do AND how well it is working.

None of the above advice is rocket science. In fact, I would consider the above a minimum effort to understand your customer's needs. However, in the daily battle to keep our heads above water, this is the kind of thing that we are all tempted to give up. We always feel that we must execute the internal communications and demands and thus we cut the customer short. If you feel that happening, let your manager know and suggest some internal things that the company can eliminate so that this important "in touch" work can be done. Without this work, you become just another selfish voice to the customer and will eventually become irrelevant.

As in the old song that says, "The head bone's connected to the neck bone...", many of our skills and competencies are connected or at least inter-related. For example, I think we can all see the relationship between the skill of Understanding Customer Needs (what I call Empathy) with the skill of Building Trusting Relationships and with the entire competency called Customer Strategy Alignment. Under Customer Strategy Alignment there is another "skill" that I think is a natural outcome of Empathy, and that is Joint Business Planning.

Whether you think that Joint Business Planning is a skill or a process, I believe it is something you will do once you have empathy for your customer. In fact, I have been doing JBP long before it was even called that, and I can attribute much of my success to this natural manifestation of empathy.

I have seen many different versions of JBP's, some better than others of course, but the good ones have three common components. They are:

-Agreed to goals – This section should include all of the numbers that are important to both parties. Volume should be one of those numbers, since it should be important to you. Share will probably not, since the customer doesn't really care whose share grows. YOU will need to make sure that the volume that you and the customer agree to will also deliver share growth for you. The other goals are up to you. They can include margin goals for your customer, inventory turns, DC service levels or even store level in-stock positions. It is up to you, but you must do your homework to make sure that you can deliver what you agree on.

-Agreed to Strategies – This is a roadmap on how you both plan to deliver the before mentioned goals. This section will drive your actions and choices through the year. It is imperative that you relate your activities to these strategies and keep your customer honest. When they make decisions that are not consistent with these strategies, you will need to remind them! You should always try to bring the shopper into at least some of these strategies. Who is their High Potential Shopper (HPS)? How do you bring them into their stores? What will that help you accomplish?

-Building Blocks – These are the major activities that you both plan to execute in order to reach your goals. These are not the same thing as your strategies, but they should be consistent with them. There should be joint ownership of these building blocks. You will, undoubtedly, own some of these building blocks and be responsible for some of this activity, but the customer MUST have responsibility in this area also.

At the end of this chapter, I have provided an example of a good Joint Business Plan. It is no particular retailer's plan and the numbers are removed, but it will give you an idea of what a good plan will look like.

Before you get carried away with warm and fuzzy feelings for your customers, it is important to remember that your primary responsibility is still to the company that employs you. For me, that company has always been Procter and Gamble. Whether you have empathy, sympathy or even disdain for your customer, you still need to deliver results for your company. The reality is that disdain will misdirect you, and sympathy can misguide you, but empathy will actually help you deliver results. If you have it naturally, you should use it, rely upon it and even try to strengthen it. If you do not have it naturally, you should develop it or at least simulate it. The effort will look the same to the customer and the results will look the same to your employer.

> **It's not the process that is important, it's the SALE !!**

Final note and opinion

In my 30 plus years with P&G, I have found that we are good at many things. We hire very bright people. We are very disciplined, as people and as a company, and for sure we have a great work ethic. There are not a lot of lazy people running around within the company. One thing we are NOT so good at, however, is simplifying things. If anything, we are good at complicating them.

Today, P&G has several processes/programs that we ask the field to use to manage the business. There is Joint Value Creation (JVC), Shopper Based Value Creation (SBVC), Joint Business Planning (JBP), Key Account Plans (KAP) and Objectives, Goals, Strategy and Measures (OGSM's) and more. Some salespeople also have Action Plans and Business Plans, and as a company we tend to reward all of this process work.

I personally don't think that all of this process work is bad. Some of it, in fact is very good. There is, however, just too much of it. It often seems to me that the goal is not to sell the shopper or the customer anymore, but to complete all of the processes. We must get our eye back on the ball and recognize that **selling** is the goal, not just completing the SBVC process (or any other) properly. Those processes and programs are only as good as their ability **to help us sell**, and when there are too many tools or processes, they actually become a hindrance to sales instead of an enabler.

In my opinion, there should be one process that we employ to drive our business and it should be called Joint Business Planning (JBP). I believe there should be an external version of this process aimed at the retailers, our customers, and this process would include a focus on the shopper and the idea of Joint Value Creation. There also should be an INTERNAL version of this process that CBD (sales) should use back with the brands to plan our business, and that process should include a focus on the shopper. You could even work the concept of OGSM's into this internal branch of a JBP process.

The beauty of this system is its simplicity. This allows more of the energy of your Sales teams to be spent against the customers, trying to figure out how to sell our shoppers. I believe this simplified system would yield more sales and thus more successful and motivated sales people, but it does require a commitment to the concept of SIMPLICITY!

FYE January 2006 (Feb '05 - Jan '06)

	Sales	Change YA	NMM$	NMM%
Year to Date (thru Q2)	$XXX,XXX,XXX	#VALUE!	$XX,XXX,XXX	#VALUE!
Projected Finish	$XXX,XXX,XXX	#VALUE!	#VALUE!	XX.X%

2005 Summary:
(3) 5-2 Drive Items Includes:
- 4 Tabs vs. 3 in PY.
- Feature Dollars $XX.X (+XX%). Original Budget proposed was $XXMM.

Strategies:
1. Jointly Create Awareness & Consumption
   - Drive New, especially in new segments.
2. Increase Transaction Size
   - Specific Items would be mentioned here.
3. Build Customer Profitability
   - Take BDF out of non-strategic price points
   - Take advantage of national OLA's.

FYE 2007   (Feb '06 - Jan '07)

Year 1 New Item Sales

		Comments
+ New Items	$xx,xxx,xxx	New Items Expected to Deliver an Incremental $xx.xMM ().
+ New Item Sales	$xx,xxx,xxx	New items for how many weeks Description of support/size of launch
	$xx,xxx,xxx	New items for how many weeks Description of support/size of launch
	$xx,xxx,xxx	New items for how many weeks Description of support/size of launch
+ New Store Growth	#VALUE! xx.x%	
+ Merchandising	$x.xxx	Incremental merchandising Goal is $xxMM (+xx%)
+ Other:	#NAME?	
	$xx,xxx,xxx	other plans or factors
	$xx,xxx,xxx	other plans or factors
	$xx,xxx,xxx	other plans or factors
SALES Budget	#VALUE!	

Help Needed from Customer
DRIVE new technology
DRIVE male segment
Run so many Tabs this year vs last
Run so many displays this year vs last
Highest level of support for certain initiatives

NMM$	NMM%
#VALUE!	xx.x%

Help Needed from P&G
Strong media plans
Trial Building plans for new items
TFI's to fund Rollbacks
OLA's on PDQ displays
A certain # of special packs this year

Key Measures

	FYE - Projected	Change YA
Comp Sales	#VALUE!	#VALUE!
Total Sales	$XXX,XXX,XXX	#DIV/0!
Initial Margin (gr chg vs YA)	xx.x%	#DIV/0!
NMM% (gr chg vs YA)	xx.x%	#VALUE!
NMM$	#VALUE!	#VALUE!
GMROII	$xx.xxx	#DIV/0!
Turns	#VALUE!	#VALUE!
Markdowns	#VALUE!	#VALUE!

	FYE - Proposed	Change YA
Comp Sales	#VALUE!	#VALUE!
Total Sales	$XXX,XXX,XXX	#VALUE!
Initial Margin (gr chg vs YA)	xx.x%	#VALUE!
NMM% (gr chg vs YA)	xx.x%	#VALUE!
NMM$	#VALUE!	#VALUE!
GMROII	$xx.xxx	#VALUE!
Turns	#VALUE!	#VALUE!
Markdowns	#REF!	#REF!

Introduction for Distribution by Jim Dobens,

William Procter Sales master – class of 2004

Introduction:

Selling Distribution is the lifeblood of what we do...it is the primary objective of the Sales Organization. Long term success in delivering year after year means that you have been successful in selling new distribution to your

customer <u>without losing something else</u>.

Distribution

(aka – Product Assortment)

Chapter 8

There has been an age old debate as to which of the Business Fundamentals is most important. The Business Fundamentals that I'm talking about are Shelf Management, Pricing, Merchandising and Distribution. In this debate, many people tout the well accepted statement, "You can't sell it if you don't carry it" to argue that Distribution is the king of these Fundamentals. Actually, if you apply the simplest interpretation of that statement, then they are probably right. If you, as a sales person, don't get your account to carry an item, list it, and put it on their shelves (however you want to define distribution), then they won't sell it to their shoppers and you won't be able to sell any of it, or ship any of it to them.

For the weak minded, the debate usually stops there. How can you get around such a strong statement? How can you compare Shelf

Management or Pricing or Merchandising to the accepted King of the Business Fundamentals, Distribution. The logic is too strong! If you don't carry it, you can't sell it. How can you argue against THAT?

But then, you need to think a little deeper to get an argument going. When you say that an account "Carries" an item, or has it in distribution, you are assuming some sort of treatment in at least two of the other Business Fundamentals, Shelving and Pricing. You are assuming that the item is on the shelf of your account somewhere, right? It may not have the best shelf position possible, but you are assuming that it is on the shelf and not in the back room of the store somewhere or, even worse, still sitting in your account's warehouse, where no customer could possibly find it.

> # You can't sell it
> # if you don't carry it.

You are also assuming that it has some sort of price attached to it. You might even be assuming that the price is not ridiculous. You are probably assuming that the price is reasonable and maybe even competitive. That is a lot of assuming. Your item is in distribution, it is on the shelf in good position, and it is priced competitively. Well, with all that assuming, I guess it is easy to proclaim that Distribution is the most important Business Fundamental

I personally think that it is more appropriate to say that the Distribution is the FIRST Business Fundamental or that the Business Fundamental process BEGINS with Distribution. All the Fundamentals are important, and for some items and at some of the retailers out there, Distribution may be the most important. For other retailers or other items, one of the other Business Fundamentals might be more important.

At this point, you are probably saying to yourself, "This is a funny way to start a chapter on the importance of Distribution." And it probably is, but I wanted to make a few points. First, ALL of the Business Fundamentals are important. Second, we shouldn't confuse the impact of one

Fundamental on others. That occasionally happens and I'll give you some examples of when it does. Third, I eventually want to make the point of when and where Distribution IS key, or most important. First let's talk about how we can confuse the impact of two Business Fundamentals.

Shelf or Distribution

Today, there are 10,000 new item launches a year in Consumer products.

> # Item proliferation has put tremendous pressure on the Retailers' shelves

In 1974, when I started with the company, Crest toothpaste offered 10 items to retailers. We had 5 different sizes and two flavors. Today, Crest offers more than 70 items for retailers to carry, and while stores have gotten bigger since 1974, they aren't seven times larger. What has driven this new item activity and what is the result?

I believe that there are three reasons for this explosion of new items. The first reason is legitimate and I will spend very little time on it. That "reason" is the consumer. Many companies, including P&G have found more and more things that consumers want and need. This is all well and good, but it can't account for all of the introductory activity. I believe there are two other reasons that are driving this growth. First, companies have found that "activity" drives volume growth for their brands. It may not grow the category, but it may steal share from competitive brands. All companies promise aggressive marketing plans (and some actually deliver them), so buyers are afraid to say no and be left behind. The buyers bring in most of the new items and center most of their merchandising plans on these new items. With all of this effort and support, the new items are often a success, even if they just trade volume from one brand to another. That brings me to the second "not so legitimate" reason that item selection is getting proliferated – buyers that can't say no! I don't know if this means that sales people are better than buyers or if it means that buying is more difficult than selling, but, in my opinion, too many items are being accepted each year by buyers across the country, and not enough existing items are being eliminated.

The result is that retail shelves are getting absolutely stuffed with their selection, and the shopping experience is getting more difficult. Go check around your local retailers, especially Drug and Food stores, and see how many single facings you see. Look in the Dentifrice section, and you will find many stores who have single facings on every item on their shelves. This should be the first warning signal that something is wrong. Think about it. This means that their very best selling item and their worst selling item have the exact same amount of shelf space. That can't be good. Either they are running out of their best item or they have WAY too much inventory on their slower sellers. Some retailers try to manage this by caring little to no inventory on those slow sellers. There are two problems with that thinking. First, this leads to sloppy looking shelves, and shoppers hate that. Second, it is still a waste of space. Whether you leave a shelf empty in the front of the shelf or in the back, it is still wasted space that could be put to more productive use.

The other result of this item proliferation is that the shopping experience becomes far more painful. I've watched shoppers in a Walmart store look for toothpaste for over five minutes, picking up packages, reading the back panels, putting them down, and then eventually throwing (literally) a tube of toothpaste in their shopping cart. This, again, can't be good.

> **When your best selling item and your worst selling item have the same shelf space – that can't be good!!**

In the book Blink, by Malcolm Gladwell, he talks about how too much information or too many choices can have a negative impact on the decision making process. He used the example of an in-store demonstration on Jams. When there were 8 brands being demo'd, the demo converted to a sale 33% of the time. When the demo was increased to include 15 brands, the conversion to sales actually went down to 15%. Does this mean that people who are shopping for toothpaste at Walmart are walking out and not buying toothpaste because they are confused and exasperated? Actually, I think that is possible, but at a minimum it is registering as a bad shopping experience.

In today's competitive world, every retailer is trying to get and keep shoppers in their stores. They do that in a variety of ways. They offer low prices. They make their checkout lines faster. They keep their stores clean. They do all of this to offer their customers a better shopping experience. I believe that the RIGHT item assortment, that walks that fine line between being too lean and too excessive, will create a competitive advantage in the future. Shoppers will gravitate to it and, since I believe most stores are over assorted, it will save retailers that get it right a ton of money.

Now, if you are selling one of those accounts whose shelf space is driven by their distribution (in other words, they have one or minimal facings on all items), you have a two pronged responsibility. First, to the company, you need to get the proper shelf space for your brands, and if that can only be done by selling in new distribution, you have to do it. Second you need to lead your account to the RIGHT assortment, which probably offers fewer items that meet the shoppers' needs and allows for multiple facings on top sellers. This will improve in-stock and the appearance of their shelves. You may even find, as you go to this new world of a "right" assortment, your account can reduce the number of items they offer to their shoppers, but their shoppers will actually believe that their assortment is greater! There is plenty of evidence that this phenomenon occurs. This will not be an easy sale, but if you make it, and apply it to ALL companies and brands on the shelf, I believe the payout for all concerned will be huge. Let me emphasize that any efficient assortment effort must be applied to all brands in the category, or you must make absolutely sure that you protect your shelf space if it is only applied to you.

When Distribution IS King

Distribution that satisfies a shopper need (or at least a "want") is almost always a good idea. Be certain, however, that you stay aware of your competitive position? You should know what *your* competition is offering and what the retailer's competition is offering. Should you follow them blindly? Absolutely not. The number of items in distribution is less important than the shopper needs that are being met or missed. Does your competition or the retailer's competition carry any items that satisfy a shopper need that you are not? That is the more important question. Let me give you an example of a brand that did a great job by identifying and satisfying a shopper need. Crest.

When I took over the Oral Care business on the Walmart Team, Crest's distribution, in terms of the number of items that it carried, was roughly equal to Colgate's. As I mentioned above, one of the first things I did was go to a Walmart store and watch their shoppers shop for Toothpaste. I was shocked at how exasperating things had gotten, and I decided that one of the things I was going to try to do was to simplify that shopping experience. But how could I do that and not lose any volume.

To find the answer, we went to the shopper decision tree. We found that "Flavor preference" was way down the list. We also looked at our distribution and found that we had several similar flavors in some of our brand segments. We had "cool" mint. We had "smooth" mint. We had "icy" mint. Sometimes we had all three in the same segment. We decided to execute a reduced assortment test, and in that test we eliminated this duplication and devoted that shelf space to the items that we decided to keep. Let me emphasize that *we kept the shelf space for the Crest brand* and just expanded the shelf space on the Crest items that we kept. The rationale for this was simple. We argued that if we had an

> **Distribution that satisfies a shopper need is almost always a good idea.**

icy mint Crest item next to a smooth mint Crest item and we eliminated one of them, virtually 100% of that volume was likely to go to the item that remained, so the item that remained would actually need more space to accommodate the extra volume. While the actual results may not be THAT clean, I am confident that virtually all of the volume would remain in the Crest brand. So, the shelf space should remain devoted to Crest.

Other brands made other choices, and what we found was that Crest's business actually got better. Crest's share in this reduced assortment test actually grew. While we did not expand this test to all stores, I did apply this learning to my decisions for all stores and I reduced the number of items in Crest's assortment relative to Colgate. Again, we kept the space for Crest and we weren't missing any real shopper needs, and our business exploded. I believe we were offering the shopper a better shopping experience through a better in-stock position and more easily understood assortment.

Then Crest launched Whitening Expressions. This was a line extension that was almost completely aimed at "Flavor". I was concerned that this would not work. After all, we had just looked at the shopper decision tree and found that "Flavor Preference" was extremely low in rank vs. the other concerns. Also, we had been eliminating flavors and our business had improved. I was skeptical, but I sold this initiative with Walmart's full support. Good thing!

Crest Whitening Expressions was a HUGE success. So doesn't this invalidate the data that we had used to eliminate items based on Flavor? Actually, no. What we found was that the company had really done its homework on Whitening Expressions. They had seen the same shopper decision tree data that I had, but had found that "Flavor" was only ranked low because there really were no choices in the Toothpaste category. When everything is a "mint" of some kind, the shopper didn't really care. However, when they actually had some exciting choices like Cinnamon and Citrus, all of the sudden flavor became much more important. The beauty of both of these examples is that we listened to the shopper and offered the assortment that she wanted. In one case we eliminated items that they didn't care about (smooth mint vs. icy mint) and we added assortment in an area that they did care about, real flavor choice. Distribution IS key when it meets a shopper need!

New Items and Initiatives

In the beginning of this chapter, I stated that it was an accepted belief that Distribution is the most important Business Fundamental. We accept that because we have always heard, "You can't sell it if you don't carry it". I spent the next few pages trying to convince you that ALL the Business Fundamentals are important and that we should just consider Distribution as the FIRST! It all starts with selling the item or the line in. Now that I have convinced you, I'm going to tell you when Distribution IS king.

I'll start with a story about a failure. When I came to the Walmart Team, I inherited an Old Spice Deodorant business that was dramatically underdeveloped. As I studied the customer profile of Old Spice and compared it to the typical Walmart customer, I found many similarities, so I decided to make Old Spice a key plank in my strategy to build our overall Beauty Care business. I couldn't see any reason why this brand should be underdeveloped and I drooled over the extra cases I could sell if I could just get this brand to the development that the average retailer around the country had. How could I lose? This was a sure thing.

Two years later, after beating my head against every Business Fundamental and doing everything I could to fix Old Spice, I was exactly where I started. The business was much bigger, but, of course, so was Walmart. All my growth was driven by theirs. My share was no better and still underdeveloped compared to the rest of the country. My only explanation was that something had happened to Old Spice when it was introduced at Walmart, and all my effort was not going to fix it. This brings me to the first time when Distribution is King – during a brand's introduction.

The other reason that leads me to that conclusion is that I have had so many experiences where successful launches have established a Brand at a high share level that extended for years. I believe that the really successful launches are sold to the shoppers, through the retailers and THIS is what gives those introductions staying power.

Maybe the best example that I can give of this phenomenon is the Pantene Shampoo introduction at Walmart. Pantene was a tiny, prestige brand that P&G picked up when we acquired the Richardson Vicks Company. It was a good solid brand, but P&G had big plans for it. Not long after I began to call on Walmart, we launched new Pantene Pro V. This was a launch designed to leverage the premium name of Pantene and make it more mainstream.

When we launched it, we convinced Walmart that it had the potential to change the complexion of the entire category. This was a mainstream, high dollar brand that had the potential to drive dollar volume and profit into the category. With this in mind, Walmart fully supported this introduction. They started this full support with - what else – Full Distribution. They also supported Pantene with good pricing, solid shelf space and position and excellent display and feature support, so it really was a total effort. But, that total effort started with Distribution. This total effort sold the Walmart shoppers on buying Pantene, and once they were converted to Pantene I was in for a very good run at Walmart as I just replenished their shoppers' purchases.

Walmart developed a disproportionately high share of the Pantene business which I benefited from for the next four years. Even today, Pantene is better developed at Walmart than it is nationally, and I attribute that development to the quality of its introduction. This is the opposite of the Old Spice example I talked about above. We launched it right and we convinced the Walmart shoppers to buy it. This is the kind of launch that can drive long term volume growth, and it starts with Distribution.

Crest is another brand that used new Distribution to drive volume at Walmart and across the country. At the beginning of new millennium (year 2000) Crest found itself in a very unenviable position. Crest's share had been declining for years and finally fallen to a distant second place share brand in the Toothpaste category behind its archrival, Colgate. Crest used a series of introductions from Dual Action to Crest with Scope to Whitening Expressions to regain the attention and loyalty of their shoppers. At Walmart we launched these introductions with quality, and within two years, we were back on top. In four years, Colgate was in the same position that we were in back in 2000. Today we are still benefiting from the superior execution of those initiatives, and I anticipate that Crest will continue to benefit for years to come, and we used new distribution to do it.

Hidden Distribution Opportunities

Believe it or not, sometimes Distribution opportunities are right under our noses. I have often fought and sold my way to new distribution and then allowed poor execution to minimize the volume impact of these new items. At Walmart, getting distribution authorized for all stores can get our items placement in over 3,000 stores. If stores mishandle their initial order or for some reason don't get an initial order, you could have stores that are authorized to carry the distribution, but are not. At Walmart, even a 5% miss will leave 150 stores without distribution. This is the size of some entire chains and a big miss.

It is extremely important to check your "authorized" distribution immediately after you have sold in any new distribution to make sure you are hitting on all cylinders. It's actually a pretty good idea to check all your items on a regular basis to make sure that the natural wear and tear of the market place doesn't take away some distribution that

> **Make sure your items are selling on all cylinders (stores).**

you should have. This is important, not only because it will give you some extra volume, but also because your buyer is assuming that each item is in all the stores that it should be in. Missing authorized distribution will increase the likelihood that the item will be misjudged and deleted.

In the old days, like when I started with the company, it would be very difficult to identify missing authorized distribution. In fact, it would probably only be identified by using a very thorough and expensive store survey. Today, with many retailers sharing their point of sale (POS) data with us, this task is much easier, but it does take discipline and the belief that your efforts will be rewarded. While I haven't kept track of all the cases that I have shipped as a result of correcting missing authorized distribution, I have to believe that it can mean a couple of index points per year. This can make the difference between finishing at a 98 index or a 100. In this example, it is two small index points, but one huge difference.

When Distribution is REALLY King – The Club Channel

The Club Channel is a unique animal. The concept was pioneered by Sol Price out in California in 1976 with a chain called Price Club. The concept was that they would charge a membership fee but then offer very low prices. The difference in their prices vs. the average retailer was (they would argue) great enough to more than cover the cost of the membership fee. This was particularly true if you bought a major appliance or tires or any other big ticket item that they carried. The savings on that one purchase was enough to compensate for the fee. Unfortunately, the repurchase cycle on tires and refrigerators can be measured in years, and they needed something to deliver the everyday traffic, so they also included some consumables in their assortment.

However, Sol was into efficiency. He used the slogan, "the intelligent loss of business" as his guide to how much assortment he should carry, especially in the consumables area. This meant that he was willing to give up some business if he felt it was too costly for him to compete for it. With this mantra, he offered very limited distribution on items that he felt offered great value and particularly appealed to small businesses. He also wanted to offer his shoppers a value for their membership fee. Since many mainstream items and sizes were being offered at very competitive prices in other retailers, he decided to offer very large sizes or multi-packs so that he could show a value on a per ounce basis. This strategy worked because most of these large sizes were not carried in the "conventional" stores, and almost all manufacturers offer a discount for their large sizes. For example, the savvy shopper would expect to pay less per ounce for a gallon of Orange Juice than they would for a quart. You can apply this same principle to pickles, shampoo and paper towels. This same strategy, more or less, is still being executed today in Club Stores across the country.

The result is an environment where distribution is king and arguably (by some people) the only Business Fundamental that you need to consider in Clubs. Today, Walmart will offer 130,000 items in their Supercenters, and over 70,000 items in their Discount stores. This compares to only 4,000 items being offered in a typical Costco store (or warehouse, as they call them). There are not many brands that have multiple items in distribution at Costco, and I would guess that for most brands, one item represents their entire assortment.

In this environment, it is easy to make the case that Distribution is king. However, even at Costco, you need to be concerned about the other Business Fundamentals. What is my price? Does it show a value vs. other retailers? Where is my pallet located (most items are merchandised on pallets in Club stores)? How does my pallet look at store level? Is it attractive to the shopper? Can I get my item merchandised in a second location (a short term display)? Would my item be responsive to an in-store demo, which is popular in Club stores?

But, let's get back to reality. Distribution is 80 to 90% of the battle in Club stores. And, once you get distribution, you are not guaranteed to keep it. All the Club stores have volume targets for their items that are pretty strictly enforced. If you get an item in, but it doesn't sell up to expectations, you could find yourself spending a significant amount of money to eliminate inventory if the item is deleted. Given this reality, it is even more important that you work back with Marketing to create items that appeal to shoppers and will give you the best chance of success in the Club environment. The need to "create" items that will appeal to shoppers may not be unique to the Club trade, but it is significantly more important there. As you go to create an item for Club, here are some questions you should be asking:

-Should I offer a multi-pack or just a single larger package? There are positives and negatives to both for the shopper and for the company.

-What should my primary packaging look like? How will I convey the benefits of my product or of my price through this packaging?

-How will my product be configured on my pallet (or tray) so that it is easy to shop for it in a club store? Do you need 4 side, 3 side, 2 side or 1 side shoppability on your pallet?

-How will I price this new item? You will want to show a value, but remember, the rest of the trade makes up 90% of your volume, and you can't disadvantage them in your effort to get Distribution in Club.

There are more questions that you have to ask, but this list will get you started. This is an exercise that you will quickly get used to. If you aren't recommending a new item at a Club store on a regular basis, you are often renewing an existing item or planning for a "Club" version of something that is being launched nationally in the conventional trade. This whole "item creating" process is a real challenge in this channel.

> **In Club stores, Distribution IS 80 to 90% of the battle.**

Finally, in the Club channel, you will be constantly fighting for partial distribution. There are some items that can be found in all Costco's, for example, but just because you can't get an item in all Clubs, does not mean that you shouldn't be trying to figure out how you can get it into SOME Clubs. Of course, your first call of duty is to get all items that can be carried in all Clubs into every Club. After that is accomplished, you need to find out which of the brands you have left deserve to be in partial distribution.

You could have an item with a particular strength in a particular geography. I remember that when we sold Jif Peanut Butter, there was a constant battle for Clubs with Skippy (Con Agra). We were constantly researching which states or Nielsen marketing areas were Jif's strongholds vs. Skippy's. Our argument was that if you were only going to carry one brand, that brand should be Jif if our brand share was higher in a particular area. In a place where Distribution really is king, getting an item in 200 of Sam's 385 Clubs was a HUGE sale. The analysis to identify Distribution opportunities for Club stores is an ongoing challenge.

The Bottom Line

Whether or not Distribution is the most important of the Business Fundamentals, I think most people who sell consumer goods products would agree that it is at least a very important first step in the Business Fundamental process. To sell in any new item or initiative you must focus on the benefits that the item or initiative will offer to the consumer (the shopper) and the retailer. No retailer is going to carry anything just because it is good for P&G.

Once the new distribution is sold in, then you have to position it for success, and that requires thorough work in the other Business Fundamentals. Get your retail price right (competitive, but as profitable as possible for the retailer). This will help you get it positioned properly on the shelf and make it easier to get merchandising support. As I state in the "Pricing" chapter, retailer profitability is the rising tide that lifts all ships. It will make it easier for you to sell all the other Business Fundamentals. Even after your new distribution is established you will need to keep a continual watch on the other Business Fundamentals to keep it. It is a cycle that, while we often complain about it, we hope it never ends.

Introduction for Leadership by Jeff Rosfeld,

Lifetime Achievement Winner – 2006

Introduction:

It's not surprising that Kevin does such a wonderful job with the topic of leadership in this book. What is surprising is that he has asked me to chime in.

I always thought it made sense to "think big". First, THINK! Take the time to think. You owe that to those who follow you. Lead with passion and compassion to a well thought through goal. And make it a BIG goal. Why do all the work for an easily achievable result? Oh yeah...and...take time to make a decision proportionate to how long it will take you to reverse that decision.

Think Big. Do well. Do good.

Leadership

Chapter 9

Margaret Thatcher once said that there were two basic categories of leaders. First, there are leaders who just try to find out where people want to go and then go and get in front of them. I'll call this "political" leadership. Take a poll. Find out what people want and then claim that as your position. No vision is necessary. No passion for any position is required. No guiding principles are needed.

The second kind of leader that Ms. Thatcher described knows where he or she wants to go, and why. These leaders have passion for their positions and principles that guide everything that they do. Their passion attracts people, and they are skilled at getting people to work HARD and work together toward a shared goal.

If you are the first kind of leader, you need not read this chapter. Take a poll and find out where your people already want to go. If you want to be like that second type of leader, then this chapter is for you. After 30 years of leading Sales Units, Districts and Multi Functional Customer Teams for P&G, I have identified what I believe are the key elements to good, successful Leadership.

The beauty of these elements is that they work whether you are leading a Sales Unit of four people, a Multi-Functional Team or running a company. You must have a vision of where you want your team to go, whether it is in business, or government, or even in sports. You must, then, get your people to buy into that vision and then make it easy for them to accomplish their parts of the total vision. Finally, feedback, especially positive, is essential. To make it easy for you to remember the road map, I've captured these four elements to successful leadership in four memorable "E's":

-Envision
-Enroll
-Enable
-Encourage

Let's talk about each of these elements separately and see how they fit together into a complete and effective plan for leadership.

-Envision

Yogi Berra is a hall of fame catcher for the New York Yankees. He is also a world famous purveyor of comical, sometimes obvious and yet profound statements. His is the one, for example, who said, "It's not over until it's over" when talking about the outcome of any sporting event. He also said, "This is like deja vu all over again." I think you get the idea! One of Yogi's most famous quotes has a lot to do with leadership. He said, and I quote, "If you don't know where you're going, you'll probably end up somewhere else!" Obvious? Kind of. Profound? Absolutely! I think Yogi was saying that we all really do have an idea of where we want to go, and it is a good place where we are successful and things are well with us.

However, if we don't commit to that vision, that plan or that goal, we could end up, well, somewhere else.

When I was coordinating the shelf analysts for the Walmart Team, I had that quote framed for each of them. This was to remind them that they needed to have a vision of what success looked like BEFORE they went into the layout room. If they didn't align to a specific vision, they would probably end up - somewhere else.

If you were to look up the word "envision" in Webster's dictionary, it would say that it means to, "Imagine; conceive of; see in one's mind" or to "picture to oneself; to imagine what is possible." This is the first step of Leadership, and that is to have a vision of what can be and what you would like to have happen. If you don't have a vision, you can be a leader in name or title, but you will not be the actual leader of your team.

> # If you don't know where you're going, you'll probably end up somewhere else.
>
> ## Yogi Berra

If you don't have a vision, get one!

I have taken over many teams in many different situations. I've taken over teams that were very successful, and I believe this is the easiest leadership situation to encounter. The best advice I can give in this situation is to NOT change things too quickly. Embrace the existing vision, direction or goals until you have a good handle on YOUR vision and until the people on your team are ready to accept a new direction. Eventually, you need to get a vision, but you need to keep the team intact while you are constructing it.

I have taken charge of teams that were a disaster. Imagine a team that has not hit its numbers for years and may have even violated some sound basic principles to put themselves in a difficult situation. This is when, whether you have a grasp of all the problems or not, you need to come up with a vision quickly, and that vision needs to revolve around the basics. I think a classic example of this strategy is when A.G. Lafley took over as CEO for P&G. A.G. told the world and all of the company's employees that we were going to return to the company of old. We were going to focus on our strengths and deliver what we had always delivered in the past.

This approach was brilliant. The employees embraced it, and the street loved it. It reminded everyone of the company's proud history and instantly gave us all confidence that we would find our way out of the problems that we were in. I'm not sure if A.G. had all of the answers the day he took over (we had a number of problems), but this return to the basics and this reminder of our heritage was a brilliant move.

You may find yourself in either of these situations or anywhere in between. No matter where you are, you can adjust the speed with which you unveil your new vision based on the success or need of your team and your ability to confidently deliver one, but remember, you must deliver one. Your vision can be expressed in a number of ways:

- It can be an actual vision statement. A vision statement is a forward looking statement that describes where you want your team to be in the future, but it is stated in the present tense.

- It can be a very solid and comprehensive Action Plan. A good Action Plan includes some sort of number (very measurable) along with the strategies and even tactics that will deliver that measurable goal.

- It can be a slogan or motto. These need to be short, crisp, memorable and extremely meaningful. I think a good motto or slogan is particularly important if you are the leader of an entire company or a large number of teammates.

Maybe the best way to explain the importance of and the effectiveness of a good slogan is to give you a couple of examples. The first example is one that was used by Tom Coughlin of Walmart to direct and motivate his entire Operations organization which included hundreds of thousands of people from Regional VP's to cashiers. Here was his slogan:

-Stock it
-Price it
-Show them the Value
-Take their money, and
-Teach them

This was a brilliant and very effective slogan for a number of reasons. First, it used their language. Second, it delivered a very simple message, and that message was that they were going to focus on the fundamentals. It also sent a message of service level to their associates. It said that Walmart was going to have their shoppers favorite products in stock and was going to make their shopping experience easy. They were going to get them in the store, make it easy to find what they wanted and get them out of the store quickly (Walmart's definition of service). It said much to many people with just a few words. Now, Tom Coughlin has had his problems since then, but I think this particular direction was brilliant.

The second example of a great, directive motto is A.G. Lafley's current slogan of "Deliver the Decade". When I first heard it, I was impressed because of how much it said to me with just a few words. To me, these three words talked about:

-Celebrating the last 5 years of successful, profitable growth that we have had.
-Reinforcing that our strategies have been working (big brands, big countries, etc.).
-Setting a goal of delivering 5 more years (something we have not done before).
-It sent me a message about the importance of volume growth, but also
-It sent me a message about the importance of profitable growth (EPS growth).

Again, it said a lot with a few words, and no matter what level you worked within the company, there were many levels of communication and direction in just three words!

Finally, you aren't the leader until you have a vision. If you don't have one, get one. You can communicate your vision through an actual vision statement, an Action Plan or Business Plan or a Slogan or all four. After you have a vision, you need to make sure that everyone on your team is on the same page, and that speaks to Enrollment!

-Enroll

If a tree falls in a forest and there is no one around to hear it, does it still make a sound? If there is a plan on a team where the Team Leader is the only person who is aware of it, does this plan actually exist? While the first question above is debatable, the second one is not. For a plan to exist, I would argue that the entire team needs to be aware of it. That's a minimum, but for the plan to be effective it would always be best if the team had "bought in" to that plan. The question is, how does one do that? Let's talk "buy in" first.

I have found that the best way for people to "buy into" a plan is to participate in the development of that plan. Yet, I'm a strong believer

> # A plan created in isolation
> # motivates no one.

that a leader needs to have a plan for his or her team based on their judgment and analysis. This creates quite a dilemma. How does a leader formulate a plan based on his or her judgment and yet allow team members to at least FEEL like they have taken part in its construction? The answer lies in a new training that P&G has deployed called Persuasive Questioning.

This technique has been around forever; we just didn't have a name for it until recently. Under the name "Persuasive Questioning" it has been taught as a selling approach. The idea is, first, to know what you want to sell, and then, rather than just present your information to the buyer, you basically get the buyer to walk him or herself through the presentation using a series of questions. For example, if you were trying to sell a buyer on changing their modular process (the way they execute their plan-o-grams), you might start with some questions like:

-Tell me how you modular process works? You'll get a lot of information with this kind of a question.

-How do you feel it works, or

-Do you ever run into any issues? Since no one's process is perfect, you will get some great data on what problems the buyer feels he has with the process.

I won't go on, but I think you can get the idea. By the time the buyer has answered all your questions, the BUYER will want to change the modular process. He or she will have sold themselves and you will have accomplished your goal. The beauty of this approach is that buyers are always more committed to ideas that they believe are theirs than any ideas they feel you have sold them.

This technique is also very effective in building "buy in" to a team business plan. Just as in the selling situation, the salesperson does not enter the situation with a blank sheet of paper and start asking random questions. There should be a well thought out plan of what a person wants to sell and what questions he should ask which will lead the buyer to where you want him to go (at this point I've decided to stop the whole "he/she" thing. In the future, when I say he, it is meant to cover both genders).

> **It is better to be an owner of a plan than a victim of it.**

The same thing is true of a business plan or a vision or slogan. The leader of the team should have a meeting with his or her entire team, if it is smaller than 10 people, or the key members of the team if it is much larger, to garner support for the team's plan of action. The leader should not enter this meeting with no thought as to direction, but should have a pretty good idea of where he wants to take that team. He should also prepare the questions that will drive his team toward the plan that he has developed. This does not mean that the leader does not listen or change his plan based on the feedback that he gets in this meeting. It simply means that a leader should have SOME idea of where the team should go and then use this meeting to enhance it and garner support for it.

If you do this right, you will have a team that feels that it is an owner of the plan rather than a victim of it. As owners, you will find that your team members will work harder than ever to realize the goals of that plan, complain less and actually be happier.

Some people might say that this approach is manipulative. And, they are at least partially correct, but so is sales in general. In sales we are always trying to persuade someone to do something. Personally, I would much rather have a leader use this approach with a team that I was on than to stuff a plan down my throat and tell me to execute it. At least I would have a chance to influence it and understand my role in it.

Persuasive Questioning training is available through the company. If you haven't taken it yet, I would suggest that you take it as soon as possible.

-Enable

In a good plan, everyone has their portion to complete or achieve. Even on some good P&G Customer Teams (like the Walmart Team), the leader has a few things to do, the Marketing Manager has a few things to do, the Finance Manager, the Analyst and so on and so on. All the team members go on their merry way trying to achieve their portions of the plan and they occasionally get together (maybe even weekly) and update each other on how they are coming. That's a pretty good team, right? Right – pretty good!

The really good leaders add a layer of responsibility for themselves called enabling. "Enabling" is knocking down walls, building bridges, providing training or equipment that will allow your team members to achieve their goals. I think Sam Walton was a great example of an enabler. Whenever Sam set goals for his organization, like increasing in-stock levels to 99% or hitting some sort of volume goal, he was putting systems in place that would help order accuracy or delivery times or building new stores that would help deliver the volume. He didn't just set the goal and say, "go out and achieve it." He was enabling his people to achieve their goals.

There are so many ways to enable your team members that it would be impossible to cover all of them in any book, but I will give you three rules that will help you become an Enabling Leader:

-First, it is the leader's role. That doesn't mean that he does all of the enabling, but he finds out what is needed and arranges for the enabling. The actual enabling could come from the Leader, other team members or outside sources, but it is the leader's responsibility to see that it gets done.

-Second, it starts with a question. Tom Muccio, retired Walmart Team Leader, used to say, "What does help look like?" You can ask, "What is getting in your way?" You can even ask, "If you were king, what would you ask for?" The question isn't as important as the asking!

-Third, you need to formalize your promise. In your business plan or action plan (or whatever you call it) you need to formally capture any enabling that you have promised.

In the end, you are responsible for that enabling. You can delegate the authority to provide the enabling to others, but you can not delegate the responsibility to enable. That is yours!

-Encourage

I'm using the word "encourage" here in the broadest possible definition. In this context it can mean the lifting up of others, but it also can mean kicking someone in the hind end, if that is what they need. I'm using the word "encourage" for a couple of reasons. First, and foremost, I am a huge believer in the power of positive feedback, and second, it starts with an "E" and thus makes my four E's much more memorable.

The idea here is that once you have provided a vision to your team, and you have enrolled them in that vision or plan, and you have even begun to do what you can to enable them, you must give them feedback. As I stated above, I am a huge believer in the power of positive feedback, and I'm not the only one. I remember Tom Muccio saying, "catch people doing something right." His point was to be on the lookout for positive things that people do, and to reinforce those things. As you do this, it is more likely that those people will repeat those activities and they will eventually become habits.

Throughout my life I have played sports of all kinds and with many coaches. In those years I've watched a lot of film. I have had coaches that

> # Try to catch people doing something right!

loved to point out the mistakes I made and run them over and over and over in front of the entire team to make their points. I have also had coaches that liked to focus on the great plays that I made (and other players) and run them over and over and over. In one way, they were equally successful. I tended to repeat whatever it was that we ran over and over and over again in the film. Of course, for one coach I was repeating the bad plays or errors that I had made and for the other coach, I repeated the great plays or great efforts that I made. Which would you like your people to be repeating?

In another way, they accomplished very different things. After the film session with the coach that was focusing on my errors, I felt like... well I didn't feel very well. I think my attitude even had a negative impact on other areas of my performance. After a film session with the coach that was focusing on my great plays and efforts, I felt GREAT, and I believe this positive feeling bled over into other areas of my game. The point is, there is HUGE power in positive feedback and a leader needs to make sure that he has a plan to ensure that this positive influence runs throughout his organization. Here are a few things that the leader should do to make sure that this happens:

-**Be an example** – People will take their cue from you. If you are positive, then they will be positive. This is more difficult than you think. I have noticed that today, especially young people, love to "slam" each other. In an attempt to be hip or popular, a leader can be lured into allowing this "slamming" and even participate in it. You need to be diligent in keeping things positive. Try to catch your people doing things right, and then let them know about it.

-**Create a formal system of encouragement** – There are a million ways to accomplish this. You can have your people nominate their teammates for recognition. You can give each person on you team a certain number of formal recognition opportunities that they can use at their discretion. You can have "on the spot" recognition, or you could do all three. The point is, make it formal, make it public and make sure it gets used.

-**Praise in Public – private – even anonymously** – I'm sure you've heard the saying that you should, "Praise in Public and Criticize in Private." I believe that is only partially true. You should praise in public and criticize in private, but you should also praise in private and even praise anonymously. Some of the most effective encouragements I have received have been very private and thus personal. I've had bosses pull me into their office and close the door to tell me how much they appreciated one thing or another. VERY EFFECTIVE ! I've had supervisors who sent me a short hand-written note doing the same thing. Also, very effective.

-**Include the Spouse in the reward** – I have had some managers send a small gift (flowers or a crystal vase) when I have been through a tough work period that kept me on the road more than usual. Sometimes I have had a boss that gave me a gift card or even a couple of movie passes with a note that encouraged me to take my wife out for a treat. Doubly effective!!

You've heard it from Chevy Chase when he said, "Be the ball!" You have heard it from a variety of golfers who have encouraged us all to, "See the putt go into the hole." There is no denying that the power of positive thinking is huge, and I'm here to tell you that positive feedback or encouragement can be the start of it in your team members. Get it started as soon as you can.

Constructive Criticism

Unfortunately, people are not perfect, and every manager will eventually have to give negative feedback or constructive criticism at some point in time. Every manager needs to know that constructive criticism is an inevitable duty that must be very carefully executed. These kinds of situations can lead to significant growth in team members when it is done well, but it can have a devastatingly negative impact if done poorly. Here are a few hints on how to manage negative feedback well:

-**Wait for a pattern to develop** – Everyone is going to trip or misspeak during a presentation. If you try to correct every mistake, you are going to bury your team in negativism and never address their real opportunities. Pick your shots. Wait for patterns to develop where a team member shows a tendency to make the same mistake on a regular basis. This will keep you from being overly negative and will help you address the real issues.

-**Plan the feedback session** – Positive feedback is easy and is hard to mess up, but constructive criticism can more easily go wrong. You need to think about what you are going to say. Start out positive, remember, you care about this person. You need to be specific about your examples and have a plan on how to make improvement. Listen to what they have to say. They may tend to make excuses, but sometimes they will bring up unknown facts or circumstances. Finally, you need to end with a positive. Talk about the person's performance WITH the new improved behavior and how great that will be.

-<u>**Criticize in private**</u> – No one likes to be criticized in public. You should try to find a private place (your office, a conference room) where you can have this session. You should try to make it so that other team members don't even know that this session is occurring.

-<u>**Expect positive results and track it**</u> – Many managers don't mind giving the criticism, but don't want to take on the responsibility of tracking the results. Your session should end with a plan for improvement. It is easy to stop there, but a good manager follows through to make sure the improvement is made. This kind of commitment will also reduce the amount of negative feedback a manager will have to give. Criticizing and walking away is worthless or worse. Pick your shots. Commit to them, and follow through!

Great Minds Think Alike

I have been using these 4 E's for about 20 years now. I used them to lead my District in San Francisco and to lead three different teams in Fayetteville. I think I could argue that we not only delivered breakthrough business results as a team, but also that the people flourished and gave great individual performances. The 4 E's work.

More recently, A. G. Lafley has outlined his 5 E's of leadership; Envision, Engage, Enable, Energize and Execute. Some of the words are the same and some are different, but what I have found, gratefully, is that the principles are practically identical. Of course, I would like to explain this by saying, simply, that great minds think alike. I didn't even know who A.G. was 20 years ago, and I'm pretty sure he didn't know about my 4 E's. Both models are just based on sound principles that many good managers have been employing for years. I would, however, encourage anyone who has not gone through A.G.'s 5 E's training to give it a try. You can't reinforce these basic leadership principles too often. Go take a look.

In Closing

In closing, I think the most important quality for a leader of people to have is that they should actually LIKE people. Abraham Lincoln once said, "If you look for the bad in people expecting to find it, you surely will." I strongly believe in that statement, and I also believe that the opposite is true. Everyone on your team will have positive attributes. If you look for them, it will give you respect and even admiration for your team members and this will help you in every aspect of leadership.

It will have a positive impact on your vision because you will want to lead your people to a better place. You will want to get their input into your vision because you will respect their opinion. You will want them to do well, so you will be willing to knock down any barriers to their performance, and your feedback will be mostly positive and appropriate because you actually like them!

The big question is, can a person learn to care about people? If it is even possible, I think the key is in a disciplined application of Abraham Lincoln's

> # If you look for the good in people expecting to find it, you surely will!
>
> ## Abraham Lincoln
> Paraphrased by Kevin Canfield

actual point. He was saying that we have to stop looking for the bad in people and we need to stop the constant "slamming" or "picking" comments about people. I'm sure Abe would say that we need to look for the good in people and be positive in our comments. If you would actually accept this philosophy as your own and WORK at it, you will, over time, become a better leader.

Introduction for Pricing by Maria Edelson,

Director, Sales Capability Development

Introduction:

Don't skip over this chapter because you think, "oh, it's just pricing – there's not much I can do with pricing." That would be a mistake. This chapter will give you four specific things you can do to influence pricing and ultimately build your business as a result. So, read on and learn "how-to" with some great examples and results! Although, "pricing is at the sole discretion of the retailer", you CAN make a difference.

Pricing

Chapter 10

Pricing is at the sole discretion of the retailer. I thought I would get that over with as soon as possible. If you work for P&G, you have probably written that phrase a few thousand times on everything from deal sheets to actual power point presentations. I'm also assuming that other Consumer Products Companies have a similar statement that they attach to all of their written communications with Customers to keep them out of legal hot water. Pricing is at the sole discretion of the retailer. Now that I have said it a second time, I somehow feel better, safer and a little warm and fuzzy. Now I think we can really talk pricing.

The reality is that "Pricing" is an important, yet often ignored business fundamental for the consumer goods business. As I stated so eloquently in an earlier chapter on Shelf Management, 80% to 95% of our business is sold off of the shelf, depending on what category you are managing.

Obviously, this says that our brands need to look their best at the First Moment Of Truth (FMOT) or where the shopper often makes her decision as to what to buy. That would mean that the location of our brands is very important, and so is the retail price. If it is soooo important, than why is it often ignored?

The first reason pricing is overlooked is that it is a little scary to deal with. There are only a few places where salespeople can get into actual legal trouble, and one of those areas is "price fixing". Since most sales people want to stay out of jail, they just don't hassle with pricing. There are ways to talk pricing legally, which we will talk about later, but most salespeople just choose to by-pass the subject to be safe.

Second, talking pricing can be a little uncomfortable. When you talk to a retailer about their retail price, you are also talking about their profit. Some people really want to avoid that conversation. When you talk pricing, you are also talking about the retailer's competitive place in the market. This also means that you need to know the current situation in the market and even be able to predict competitive reaction to your suggested retail. Since no one likes to be wrong, they just skip it.

Pricing is at the sole discretion of the retailer

However, instead of just talking about why we don't talk pricing, let's talk about WHY we should and HOW we should talk about it.

Pricing can sometimes make a HUGE difference in how well a product sells. "DUH" you all say, but be careful. I'm NOT saying that the lowest price is always best, and I AM saying that some downward pricing moves don't pay off or can even have a negative impact on an item's volume. Let me give you a couple of examples.

Tide is the best selling Laundry Detergent. It certainly is not the cheapest. This should tell you a couple of things. First, the lowest price does not always win. People are intentionally buying Tide and paying more for it. Second, this would tell you that people BELIEVE that Tide is worth the higher price. Now, the decision as to what P&G will charge the retailers for Tide is made in Cincinnati, and it better be right. They need to decide if a product is going to charge a premium price or an economy price or somewhere in between (mid tier). They need to know if the product offers sufficient extra value to charge a more premium price. While we in the field don't make that decision, we should certainly be ready to give our input once we see and experience the product. We often have the best knowledge of what is going on in the market and need to express an opinion when we believe we are not priced right vs. our competition.

We did this with our Crest Toothbrush brand. While I was on the Walmart team we noticed that our Manual Toothbrush brand was in the middle of a slow but steady decline. We looked at our distribution and found it to be more than adequate, and our shelf space was probably better than we deserved. Since this category didn't receive much display support, and over 90% of our volume was done from the shelf, we had to conclude that our pricing was a problem, and it was.

We performed a fairly extensive study of the attributes offered by all the toothbrush brands at Walmart (like ergonomic handles or angled brushes or angled heads, etc.). We then compared these attributes with the retail prices and we found that we were offering fewer attributes but charging higher prices. While a brand name like Crest can afford to do this for a while and people will buy the name, over time this is not going to be a successful strategy. You have to OFFER more if you are going to CHARGE more. We shared our findings with Cincinnati and lo and behold, they actually changed their pricing strategy. This just goes to show, that while setting the primary pricing strategy is not the job of field sales, we need to give input when we believe that strategic pricing errors have been made.

So, what is the field's responsibility in the area of pricing? There are four areas where the field can have meaningful influence on pricing. They are:

1. Making sure our items are priced right vs. our competition.
2. Making sure our items cross meaningful price barriers when possible.

3. Making sure our Customers are making sufficient profitability.
4. Managing short term pricing activity that can impact the market.

Us vs. Our Competition

Within P&G, I believe that our Paper Products group and our Laundry Detergent Products group are the best at insuring that our products are priced competitively vs. OUR competition. This expertise starts in Cincinnati. These categories have done extensive research to identify the pricing sensitivity of their brands. In other words, they know how much of a delta (difference) our brands can afford to have vs. competition before the shopper begins to choose them vs. us. This is a measurement of how much better the shopper "believes" our brands are vs. others. If your categories have done this research, and you are not using it, shame on you. If it hasn't been done, you need to get the categories to do it or do it yourself through some tests in the market.

I don't think that it is a coincidence that the Paper and Laundry sales folks are also the best at staying on top of these opportunities with their customers. I can only speak for the Walmart Team, but I would say that sales attention to everyday pricing in these categories borders on the religious. They are good at it, and it pays off handsomely since in many of these categories 95%+ of their business is done off the shelf every day.

Meaningful Price Barriers

This area is clearly not rocket science, yet many of us still miss opportunities to make small but meaningful pricing moves for our brands. Have you ever seen a car advertised at $10,001? How about a house selling for $100,001? The same principle applies to Consumer Goods. Changing an electric toothbrush retail from $100 to $99 or a Laundry Detergent price going from $10 to $9.97 can deliver significant

> # Have you ever seen a house advertised for $100,001 ?

results. Even when your item is priced below $10, it can be significant to break any dollar barrier.

When I was selling our Shampoo and Conditioner business at Walmart, we had just purchased the Pantene Brand from Richardson Vicks and were restaging it. We had a 15oz size of shampoo and conditioner which I had retailed at $3.17, and things were actually going fine. Don Harris, who eventually became an Executive VP for Walmart, was the Divisional Merchandising Manager (DMM) that my buyer reported to. Don came to me and said that my $3.17 price point was the stupidest (if that's a word) everyday retail he had in his department. He challenged me to use some of my marketing funds to lower his cost so that he could lower his retail to $2.97 everyday.

Believe it or not, I originally said no. I liked the profitability that Walmart was making at $3.17 and I've always been a bit of a Scrooge with my marketing funds, so I refused to make the move. Don kept after me, and after a week or so, I finally relented. Of course, I predicted that it would make no difference (or at least not enough to warrant my investment) and that we would never be able to take the price back up. Unfortunately, or fortunately, depending on your perspective, Don was right. Pantene's business reacted immediately. My everyday business off the shelf jumped by over 10%. This more than paid for my investment and I had to apologize for my doubt. That was a little hard for me.

The point is, look for the little pricing changes that can make a big difference in your everyday business. If you aren't sure of the impact and are concerned that you won't be able to change the price back if it turns out badly, then do a test. Most buyers will agree to that sort of low risk, low work and high potential reward activity. Do it! You may be surprised and get a big bump in your business for very little investment.

Customer Profitability

I like to call customer (Trade) profitability "The Rising Tide That Lifts All Ships". When the customer's profitability is right, then everything you do gets easier. It is easier to sell new distribution. It is easier to have a positive impact on the shelf. It is easier to sell display support for your brands if the Customer feels good about their profit.

This does not mean that you have to supply the highest profit for the category. In fact, for the leading brands in any category, it would be insane to try to get to the category's average profit. Leading brands are, by their nature, very competitive. The shopper usually has a very good idea of what represents a good price for these category leaders, so to error on the high side on these items would send a negative message to shoppers. That message could make shopping visits a negative experience for the people who buy those brands, but more importantly, it could drive shoppers away permanently. However, you can also go too low. Let me give you an example.

When I was managing the Oral Care business on the Walmart Team, Crest Toothpaste had a pretty severe profit issue. The brand profit in total was just about flat lining (if you know what I mean) and some items were actually under water. This was putting tremendous pressure on the other business fundamentals.

Customer profitability
is the *Rising Tide*
that lifts all ships!!

As you can imagine, the buyer was not overly excited about stacking massive display quantities in the stores that they might even be losing money on, and shelf space and position was difficult to maintain. Most importantly, Crest's share at Walmart had fallen below national levels, and we were a distant second to Colgate.

One of the first things I did was to put together a plan to improve Crest's profitability for Walmart. At the time, this was a bold and slightly risky move. After all, how does P&G benefit from Walmart's increased profitability? In our new "payout" spending environment, where every expenditure needs to be rationalized to show a certain payout, a direct payout was difficult, if not impossible, to show. I was counting on an improved attitude towards Crest to pay off in the long run across all of the Business Fundamentals, and it did.

Over the next four years, Crest's profitability at Walmart improved even beyond the buyer's expectations, and as predicted, the attitude towards Crest changed. We made improvements in every business fundamental, but the most dramatic and effective were the changes we made on the shelf. You can read about that in the chapter on Shelf Management.

Now, over those four years, a lot happened in addition to our focus on profitability. Crest had a series of product introductions that were very effective and successful. However, each of these initiatives were even more successful at Walmart than they were nationally, and our Crest shares at Walmart went from a position slightly below the national average to a position WELL above the balance of the market. By the end of this period, not only was Crest the #1 toothpaste at Walmart, but we had a significant lead over Colgate. However, this was NOT true for the rest of the country. Said another way, Crest shares grew relative to the balance of the US. I contribute much of that relative growth to our strategy of improving Walmart's profit on Crest.

Now, you are going to ask, "How did you do that?" Good question. When I took over the business, virtually all of our Brand Development Funds were invested in every day retails. In other words, Walmart earned our funds upon purchase and invested it in their every day costs. For the record, I don't believe that is a good strategy, especially if you apply it blindly across all SKU's. Sometimes, when you do that, it ends up moving a retail from $3.17 to $2.97, like in the Pantene example that I discussed previously. In that case, it could be a good idea. But sometimes, when you blindly invest your money in an everyday retail, you lower your price from $3.87 to $3.77. THAT, is a waste of money. The shopper will never notice the difference. I believe THAT money can and should be spent more strategically.

One of the first things I did with the buyer was to get his agreement to take funding out of everyday costs if they had no strategic impact, like the second example above. This allowed us to accumulate an investment fund that we later applied back against the business, often in profit augmenting activities. We were also careful with our feature pricing to make sure that we weren't driving profitability out of the category and we used special packs to take the pricing pressure off of our regular items. That kind of merchandising activity certainly helped our profitability, but the most important move we made was to take much of our Brand Development funds out of our everyday pricing.

I strongly believe that if you invest your funds in everyday pricing, in effect reducing your list price every day, that money will eventually reduce every day retails as well as costs. In other words, you've flushed it down the toilet. I don't blame the retailers, like Walmart, for doing that either. It is in their DNA, especially at Walmart. They convince you to give them the money every day (to ensure that they earn it all) and in year one they promise all kinds of merchandising support in addition to coax you into making the commitment, but beware of year two. In year two, you can't take your funds back out of their price because that would be like a price increase across your entire business, so the retailer just assumes that as their new list price, and then they'll say,

> **Don't blindly invest your funds in every day list costs. Invest in strategically important retails.**

"Now, I need more money to give you your merchandising support." But you have no more money because you've given it all to them in their every day costs. So, you slowly lose merchandising support and watch your retails and profit margins slowly waste away.

Manage your money! Use your funds strategically on activities that are good for both you and your customer.

Managing Short Term Pricing

Nothing happens in a vacuum, especially when you are calling on Walmart. Running a feature at a wildly low price usually feels good in the short term. You sell a lot of product and get lots of attention from your company and your customer, but you also have to consider the long term impact. If you are managing Walmart's business when you do it, the whole world sees it immediately and reacts quickly. If you are working with a customer that Walmart watches (which is a lot of retailers), Walmart will notice and react. Either way, you must constantly consider the long term impact of your pricing moves on the total market.

Now, this is not always easy because, "pricing is at the sole discretion of the retailer!" But there are a few things you can do:

1. Make sure your recommendations are responsible. They should be not only mindful of the retailer's objectives, but also of market dynamics.
2. When, and if, your customer suggests some potentially damaging pricing moves, you must make sure they understand the possible long term implications of those moves.
3. If you are aware of pricing activity that you believe is not in the best interest of your business and of the customer's business, you can refuse to fund it.

This last point takes a lot of guts, and I would make sure that I get the complete support of your management before you do it, but it's that kind of courage that will deliver the best results for all concerned.

In Closing

While pricing is indeed at the sole discretion of the retailer, it is our responsibility to help them manage this area. You shouldn't and can't make the decision to create or change a price. The retailer does have complete power and responsibility to set their own prices, but we should be ready and willing to play the role of consultant in this area.

Every buyer should be aware of his or her company's objectives and know how their pricing strategy can contribute to reaching their goals. If they aren't aware, you need to help them with that understanding. There is nothing wrong with counseling your accounts in the area of pricing. You need to make sure that they know where they are vs. their competition. You need to help them think through pricing moves that they may be considering. What will be the impact on the market? What are some of the possible reactions to their move? Is this pricing move consistent with their own company's objectives and philosophies? You cannot make the decision for them; you are just making sure that they make the decision with all the best information available.

Finally, remember who you work for. It is your responsibility to manage your pricing and the funds you use to affect it, responsibly. Be thoughtful and strategic in your choices. The money you waste today can't be invested in any activity tomorrow.

Introduction for Negotiation by Rick DeVries
Category Development Manager Master – 2009

Introduction:

Learning how to negotiate is not easy – and can be uncomfortable for some of us. But learning how to negotiate is critical to a successful career in selling. Kevin is spot on in his outline on learning how to be an effective negotiator:

1. *Preparation – we have to understand not only our situation, but the situation of the buyer*
2. *Execution – Negotiation is a craft that most of us have to learn*
3. *Relationships – Being aware of their point of view*

Somebody once gave me a lesson on being prepared. He said to think of the 5 "Ps": Prior Preparation Prevents Poor Performance. In negotiation, preparation is so important. Having a good understanding of not only your objectives and limits, but also knowing the situation of the buyer and his/her point of view will put you in a position to achieve a win-win outcome.

Negotiations

Chapter 11

What is the first thing that comes to your mind when you think of "Negotiations"? Is it a person? Is it an occasion where you did your best (and or worst) negotiating? For me, it is the argument about "nature vs. nurture". You know how this argument goes. Do we inherit all of our talents and characteristics from that combination of our parents' qualities (nature) or do we develop our skills and abilities through our environment and experiences (nurture)? Are great negotiators like Henry Kissinger (President Nixon & Ford's version of Condoleezza Rice), Donald Trump and Mark Steinberg (Tiger Wood's agent) born great negotiators or do they become great?

Many people believe that the most important influence we have on our children is the genes that we bequeath them. Great athletes are just born fast and with great hand-eye coordination. Look at Michael Phelps. His body was built to swim. He has an extremely long torso and relatively short legs. He has amazingly broad shoulders and long arms. We all heard throughout the Olympics how he was built to swim. So, you could say he was at least genetically predisposed to be a great swimmer. There are many things we can be genetically more likely to become. In addition to athletics, I believe at least part of intelligence is genetically driven, and even some social tendencies can be genetically predisposed. Many believe that alcoholism, gambling, and even unfaithfulness are genetically directed.

But, there are also choices and experiences and environment that I believe can have an impact on all of these conditions. Let's look at Michael Phelps again. You can be built with that same body and never experience early success and choose not to spend hundreds of hours per month in the pool, and you can end up a funny looking department manager at Kroger. While some people might have a tendency towards alcoholism or gambling, people still have to make choices to succumb to those temptations. I think the same is true for the great negotiators.

Now, what kind of attributes will make you genetically predisposed to be a great negotiator? First, you need to be intelligent with the ability to think quickly. Being fundamentally sound in mathematics doesn't hurt. Second, you need to be generally comfortable with people. It is nice to be able to put people at ease and stay even keeled yourself. Finally, you need to be comfortable when taking a risk. When you are negotiating it implies that you are in a win or lose situation, and it takes a steady nerve to be able to stay calm even when you have a chance of walking away empty handed.

We could have a great debate on whether these qualities are inherited or learned, but I think we would all agree that no matter how we acquired these qualities, they are nice to have if you are going to be a great negotiator. The good news is that all of us tend to have some or all of these qualities naturally to some degree. The other piece of good news is that there are skills that you can acquire or learn that can enhance any natural traits that you might have to become a solid negotiator.

Now, no book, this one included, can give you the natural gifts you need to be a truly great negotiator, and even people who are born with all the advantages will not necessarily become great at negotiating without building on those qualities through diligent hard work. Back to Michael Phelps, he was born with some pretty amazing physical qualities, but he combined that with hours of hard work in the pool learning solid techniques and building his stamina to become the unbelievable swimmer that he eventually became. So, the focus of this book will be to enhance whatever natural skill set you have to make whatever you have, better! If you have it all, you could be great. If you don't, you can still become good at it and you need to remember that while negotiating is a part of selling, it is not the only part. Negotiation is only part of your selling arsenal, and you need to refine that skill as much as you possibly can.

When you analyze a person's ability to negotiate, it can be a little like analyzing a person's golf swing. There can be a hundred things to think about. But, when you are swinging a golf club, it's impossible to think of a hundred things and still actually hit the ball! There are three things you CAN do, however, that will get you most of the way home. First, keep your head down and your eye on the ball all the way through impact. Second, keep your left arm straight so that your swing will bring your club head back to where it started. And third, follow through. So, what are the three things that you can learn that will get you most of the way home in learning how to negotiate?

-Preparation
-Execution
-Relationships

Preparation

If you would read Warren Buffet's book The Snowball, you would discover that Warren was not naturally gifted at establishing personal relationships. He took Dale Carnegie courses to help himself in this area, and worked hard at applying the principles, but even today he would have to admit that he has at best unusual relationships with the people around him in his life and he is not the life of every party he attends. He is not naturally gifted with people, which is one of the skills I suggested was important to be a great negotiator.

Yet Warren owns 30 different companies and is one of the richest men in the world, no matter what the market is doing. He has brought unions to their knees and even gone toe to toe with the US government and came out on top. How did he do all of this? Preparation!!! The reason why I love to use Warren as an example of a great negotiator is because he supports both sides of the nature vs. nurture argument AND it offers an excellent example of the importance of and the effectiveness of good preparation.

Preparation is the one thing that Warren did VERY well before he bought any company, bought any stock, or negotiated with anyone. In fact, if you look at how Warren negotiated his most important purchases or compromises, he was a two-step negotiator. He did excellent research on each situation, then he made one offer and (as the book says) then he Buffetized his opponents. He never countered their offers. He just repeated his original offer until they conceded or he was forced to walk away. Most often, his opponents conceded because Warren's offer was on the mark due to his incredible preparation.

Good Preparation is something that anyone can do and it will significantly improve your negotiation results. So, how do you prepare for your negotiations? On the next page you will find a Strategic Negotiations Planning Guide that will help you methodically go through the planning process when you anticipate that you may have to negotiate on a particular proposition. While every part of this process from Background Information to Planning the actual meeting is

Strategic Negotiations Planning Guide

1. Background/Environment (What is background? What are my objective/interests? What issue do I need to solve?)

```



```

2. Relationship (Do I/how do I need to strengthen my relationship with the Other Party to negotiate more effectively?)

```



```

3. Strengths-Weaknesses (What are my key strengths and how can I take advantage of them? What are my key weaknesses and how can I defend against them? What value do I bring to the table?)

```



```

4. Goals (What are my key goals? What are targets and limits for each goal? How can I argue for my targets and limits?)

Target:_____   Limit:_____

5. Options (What options do I have? Which seem best? What is my best alternate option to making this deal?)

```



```

6. Questions (What questions do I need to get answered, or defend against, to negotiate more effectively?)

```



```

7. Meeting Plan (Where/how should I negotiate? What agenda should I follow? What roles will people on my team play? What tactics should I use and when/how should I use them?)

```



```

This Negotiation Plan filled-in by: _____ on _____

important, the most important part of your planning can be found in the center of the page, step four – establishing your goals.

For any negotiation, your goal is to land somewhere between your target and your limit. Your target is where you would like to end up after the negotiation and your limit is that place which you cannot go beyond. You will also need to remember that your buyer's target and limit will be in opposition to yours. In other words, your buyer's target will be to identify your limit, and your target will be to identify the buyer's limit. The common space between your limits is defined as your bargaining range. Now, is that as clear as mud? Since a picture is worth a thousand words in this case, I have supplied an illustration of this phenomenon.

Seller					Buyer
		Target			
		Limit			
Bargaining					Bargaining
Range					Range
		Limit			
		Target			

Part of your preparation is to identify your buyer's limit, and another part should focus on how to raise it and thus expand your bargaining range. So, what could you address that would cause a buyer to raise the price he or she was willing to pay for a product?

132

Company goal – Will your idea help them reach their goals?

Personal goals – Will your concept make that buyer look good and possibly help his or her career?

BATNA – Best Alternative To a Negotiated Agreement.

Part of being successful is being able to recognize and take advantage of your strengths, and for salespeople preparation is our strength. To illustrate this point I want to tell you a story that was told me by another savvy P&G sales veteran from the Walmart Team, Tom Verdery.

Tom was once talking to a P&G salesperson who had once worked as a buyer for a retailer, who will go unidentified. This is, surprisingly, a very unique profile in CBD at P&G and delivered some very unique perspective. The X-buyer was talking to Tom about his experience in negotiating with salespeople. He was making the point that buyers go through the negotiation process up to six times a day with different sales people and that gives him tons of practice at identifying and using the different negotiation tactics (my top 10 favorites are listed at the end of this chapter). Since salespeople only get to practice this process two or three times a month, he believed, and I agree, that it is unlikely that sales people will be better at recognizing and utilizing these techniques. Negotiating tactics are clearly a strength for buyers.

However, while making this point, he also exposed a challenge that all buyers face. While they do meet with sales people 15 to 20 times a week and negotiate in almost every call, they have little time to prepare for these negotiation sessions. In fact, he admitted that most times his preparation for these sessions consisted of the time it took him to walk from one appointment to the next. The point is, while buyers may have an advantage in the tactics used in the negotiating battle, WE clearly have an advantage in PLANNING for that battle. Many a battle has been won, even against a better equipped opponent, because of a superior battle plan. Planning is your advantage. Make sure you take advantage of your advantage!!

Execution

There are many negotiation tactics that you can use in a session to help you bargain with your buyer. There are so many recognized tactics, in fact, it is unlikely that you will use all or even most of them (again, see the end of this chapter for my personal top 10). If you are like most sales people, or even like me, you will gravitate to two or three tactics and get really good at using them. Some of my favorites are:

-Time pressure
-Need to get approval from Cincinnati
-Concede on low priority items

I'll bet you thought that when I talked about "Execution" I was going to tell you which of these techniques were the best and maybe even how to use them. That would probably take a whole book to do justice to this subject. For now, just pick out a few that you think you would be comfortable with, and PRACTICE. The good news is that I am going to give you something even more important and less known. There are three rules that you need to follow that, I believe, will drive 80% of your success in negotiations. Those three rules are:

1. Never make the first offer.
2. When they make the first offer, laugh (or at least do something that signals that their offer is outrageous, no matter how close it is to your target), and
3. Be able and willing to walk away.

Many of you will say that you HAVE to make the first offer because you have a list price for any new item and an existing price for items already in distribution. That is true, but you have to consider that as the sticker on a car window. Now, I'm not exactly sure how many cars are sold at sticker price, but I CAN say that I have never bought a car for sticker price. Your list or existing price should be considered a starting point, but not the first offer.

Whether it is for a new item or some sort of promotional program, you should try to get some direction (first offer) from the buyer through a series of questions. I would suggest you review the Persuasive Questioning material to help here, but you may want to start by asking them about their goals or objectives for their company, department, or the event that you are trying to become part of. What are they trying to achieve? Is it volume driven or margin driven? As you gather information and refine it, you may uncover a first offer or at least position yourself to ask the follow up probes that will lead to it. Don't be afraid to ask directly, "What kind of margin requirements do you have?" Once you get the response you are looking for, you need to react to it in a way that will move the negotiations to your favor.

> **Never make the first offer**

The final plank of this three-part execution strategy is the "Walk Away". If you never say no, you are probably not utilizing your funds to their greatest benefit. You also send your buyer the message that you have limitless funds. The reality is, you do not! Your funds are finite and sometimes even if you are staying within your total fund limits, you can agree to investments that do not deliver a satisfactory return for the company. Obviously, walking away from a negotiation will not deliver volume for you today, but I will suggest that it will deliver positive results in the future. YOU, however, must be the person who decides when saying no is the right answer. Generally speaking, it will be when you are operating below your limit and are in danger of setting a bad precedent for the future.

If you want to actually see this three-step approach in practice, you are in luck. There is a reality program on TV right now called "Pawn Stars". This is a show about three men who own a Pawn Shop in Las Vegas, Nevada. As you can imagine, these guys negotiate for a living, and they use this three-step process almost exclusively as their approach, including the "walk away" when they really can't get a profitable deal. If you can't catch the show, just look them up on the Internet. They have complete episodes on their site.

Now, no matter what techniques you use to negotiate with your customers, you will always be operating in a delicate area because you need to be considering the final plank of "Preparation, Execution and Relationships".

Relationships

We all need to remember that negotiating with Walmart or any other member of the retail trade is different than negotiating for a car or for a house. We may buy a car every five years or so, and houses even less often. On top of the length of time between purchases (thus between negotiations) we rarely buy the next car or house from the same person. In these situations, it is probably best for you to get the very best deal for yourself as you can and assume that the other party is taking care of their own interests. Outside of lying or cheating, which I NEVER recommend, you should get the lowest price possible and not look back when the deal is done. Things are different when you deal with the retail customer.

> # Planning is the Sales Person's biggest Advantage

While on the Walmart Team, I saw the buyer in person at least once every two weeks and talked to them or someone on their team on a daily basis. This is true for most retailer teams and we, the salespeople, get to know these people pretty well. We get to know them well on a business basis for sure, but we can even get to know their personal situations. So, versus buying a house, the length of time between contacts is days instead of years and it is not only likely, but certain that you will deal with the same person, sometimes for years.

So, how do you negotiate in THAT environment? At this point, the first thing you need to do is to re-read chapter 7 of this book on Empathy.

That is going to be the key to success in long-term negotiations with any retailer.

You will need to come up with "win - win" results of your negotiations. In order to accomplish this, you will also have to do a thorough job of - PREPARATION. You'll not only need to know what YOUR Limits and Targets are, but you will need to know what your customer's Limits and Targets are, or at least what their limits are. This will establish what that "bargaining range" is. If you can land in that area, your idea will be acceptable for all concerned AND deliver positive results for both sides.

Finally, you can negotiate agreements that fall within the bargaining range, but don't help your customer reach their goals. Part of your preparation should be to insure that what you are even planning to negotiate on is worth the effort for both sides. Does this idea help you reach your goals? Does it deliver the volume you need to reach your goals with an acceptable return for the investment dollars you will spend? Does this idea help deliver against your customer's goals? What are their current goals? Are they volume driven now? Do they need profit? Margin or Dollars of profit? Do they need customers? If you successfully negotiate an agreement to your idea will it help both companies reach their goals?

> ## If you never say "no" then you aren't negotiating

Nature vs. Nurture

If you were born with some God-given attributes that naturally make you more comfortable in negotiations, that's great. If you are more comfortable with people, if you work quickly with numbers, you have a head start, but even you should work at sharpening that skill. If you aren't a natural, you can still become a great negotiator.

No matter who you are, the key is to deliver ideas over time that fall in the bargaining range and help your customer achieve their goals. Be prepared for every negotiation. Practice and continually improve your use of the classic negotiation techniques, and finally, consider your customer's limits so that you can deliver "win-win" solutions.

My Personal Top 10 Negotiation Tactics

Tactic	Description	Examples
1) Never make first offer	Wait for Buyer to establish a first position or simply ask the buyer what is needed to come to agreement.	So, what kind of margin do you need in order for us to get this feature?
2) Laugh at the buyer's first offer	Laugh or make some extreme response when your buyer tells you his or her first offer of a solution.	Actually laughter or even an astonished look, or Wow! There's no way I can hit that number.
3) Backward Negotiating	Start from your desired final result or target	I need an action alley display to justify this spending. What can we do to guarantee that kind of support?
4) Pause	Remain quiet. This can make the buyer talk to fill the silence. This can be tricky and uncomfortable. Be prepared to move to another tactic if it exceeds reason.	
5) Deadlines	Set artificial or real deadlines to motivate fast action	If we are going to be able to produce the displays we want, I will need to get quantities to manufacturing today.
6) Limited Authority	Say you have to go to your boss to get approval for this investment. This allows you to put some cooling off time in the negotiations and return with a counter offer.	That's a lot of money and beyond my budget. I'll have to go to the team leader to see if we qualify for some investment funds.
7) What if / Suppose Questions	Ask hypothetical questions, without commitment or direction, to brainstorm possible options/alternatives	What if I gave you 2 sampling days per store, would you bring in the Pre-assembled displays?
8) Full Disclosure	Share openly with the other party to get them to share openly with you. Trust is a must!!	BDF is available to all our buying customers and managed equitably. Your competitors are on the same BDF program and accrue funds based on their actual purchases.
9) One More Thing / Nibble	Add a small concession at the end of the negotiation to take advantage of the other party's desire to close.	This promotion event will be awesome! I will need to get displays in 2,000 stores. We're already at 1,750 so that is a small increase.
10) Walk Away	Pack up your brief case and prepare to walk away. You can show some emotion if appropriate and if you can handle it. This is not a tactic you can you often. Be choiceful.	There is no way we are going to come to an agreement, even though I have tried. Call me if you change your mind.

Introduction for WWOD by Dave Geissler,

William Procter Sales master – class of 2006

Introduction:

P&G understood the power of ownership early and designed an innovative profit sharing structure in which employees truly are owners in the company while making a strategic choice to hire and train individuals with passion, values and a desire to succeed.

The daily decisions by individuals and teams within P&G may not seem important in such a large company, but the power comes from the compounding of those decisions across functions, teams and business units around the world. The result is a world class organization of people and brands that has been delivering leadership results for over 170 years.

This culture of passionate ownership thrives in our Customer Business Development (CBD) function as we serve our customers and consumers while building brands that can win at the first moment of truth. We use multifunctional teams to partner with our key customers to understand their shoppers and to develop winning business plans utilizing our leadership brands to grow mutually profitable sales and market share.

WWOD

(Act like an owner)

Chapter 12

Have you ever been in a restaurant ordering a hamburger platter that comes with french fries when you decide to do the semi-healthy thing and ask if you can substitute a baked potato for the fries, only to have the server say no, or roll their eyes and say yes like you were asking them to change the rotation of the earth? Have you ever been to a retail store having difficulty finding what you want? When you finally find an employee, they give you an indifferent shrug or an unsatisfying answer, or both. I have been in both of these situations, and I have to admit, I have been there more often than I would like to admit. In these kind of disappointing situations, I usually walk away saying, "Obviously, this person does not have a vested interest in this business" or "I bet they would act differently if they were the owner."

Now, have you ever been in those same situations and asked these questions to an owner? If you have, you would probably find that you get very different responses. In the first situation with the baked potato, you are probably going to get an "absolutely, yes", as long as the restaurant actually serves baked potatoes. They may even tell you that you have to pay a little extra in an almost apologetic fashion, but you will get your baked potato and you won't feel belittled for asking. In the second situation, the owner may not know where every item is in the store, but that person will either find it for you, or they will find someone who can. It's interesting how your attitude and actions change when you are the owner.

Recently P&G updated its PVPs (Purpose, Values and Principles). You would think that with something as basic as Purpose, Values and Principles the company would not change them very often and not very dramatically. As soon as I heard of this update, I wanted to look and make sure that one of our Values did not change, and indeed, it had not. Our Values were still – Integrity, Leadership, Passion for Winning, Trust, and OWNERSHIP.

When I started with the company, I was encouraged early and often to "act like an owner". I was encouraged to spend the company's money like it was my own and to make decisions as if I owned the company, because owners have a deeper understanding of how their actions impact the company and

> **Having a vested interest in any enterprise will dramatically change your attitude!**

a deeper concern for the company's well being. While all of our values are important, I believe that this one value is at the heart of our past success and will be at the center of the company's future success as well. If we can get every employee to act like an owner, I'm confident that our future will be secure. Certainly our profit sharing program will encourage our people to "feel" like owners. This is especially true for people who have been with the company long enough for their profit sharing to accumulate significantly. However, feeling like an owner and acting like one can sometimes be very different. And, for our young people, it is easy to say "act like an owner", but they may not know what that means. So, for those savvy veterans who are beginning to "feel" like an owner, and for those newcomers who want to know how to translate that direction into action, I decided to devote a chapter to this subject. The question became, "What Would an Owner Do?" (WWOD).

As I looked to answer that question, I found that the answer was right under my nose. I actually knew three men who owned their own successful businesses. They obviously knew how to act like owners. All I needed to do was to interview these three men and try to identify the common themes that contributed to their success. Then, since I have been working for P&G for 30+ years, I could translate that into P&G terms. Let me tell you about the three men I talked to and their businesses.

Dave Godwin – Marketplace Grill

Dave is a graduate of The University of Arkansas and of the Dallas Theological Seminary. Dave has always been a bit of an entrepreneur. After college, he went into the vending machine business in Little Rock and after a short stint as a managing pastor for Fellowship Church in that same city; he was part of the startup of a new restaurant in Fayetteville, Arkansas. Even as that endeavor was flourishing, Dave left that group to start up his own restaurant concept called the Marketplace Grill.

He started the Marketplace Grill in 1994 with a single restaurant in Springdale, Arkansas. Today, 13 years later, he has seven restaurants under that umbrella, which deliver over $12 million a year in sales. His company employs over 400 people and he has 30 managers that help him deliver his results. The Marketplace Grill stands for good food, at a reasonable price (not cheap), with great service.

Mike Rethlake – Southside Marathon

Mike is a Hoosier from Kokomo, Indiana. He's the kind of guy we all want to be; hard working, humble, kind and smarter than he gives himself credit for. Mike started working for his dad, Vern, at this same service station when he was 10, washing cars. He continued to work for his dad at night and on the weekends throughout high school. Upon graduation, he moved to full time. Today he's been there for 40 years.

In 1978 Mike bought out his father's partner and became the co-owner of the station with his dad. In 1993, Mike bought his dad's portion of the business and became the sole proprietor, but he was still leasing the building and most of the equipment from Marathon. In 2003 he bought the business from Marathon and is now the outright owner and manager of the business. 50 years ago there were about 30 "service" stations in Kokomo. A service station needs to be defined as a gas station that delivers service, like oil changes, engine repair, tune ups, etc. Today, Southside Marathon is the only "service" station left. Mike's business is thriving, and he has been at the helm for almost 30 years now.

Earl Hogan – Hogan & Associates

Earl Hogan was born and bred in Kansas City, Missouri. He is a graduate of Notre Dame University and a former naval officer. He is a voracious reader and one of the most disciplined men I have ever met. At age 70, he still works out (with free weights) at least four times a week and looks like he could be in his mid fifties. He has an incredible work ethic and has impeccable judgment (he married my sister Jo Marie).

In 1985 he started his own direct marketing business after working for a large advertising agency in St. Louis for five years. Eight years later his company employed 15 full time employees and was so successful that it was acquired by Sprint. Consistent with his character, Earl made sure that the acquisition included full time employment for all of his people, and lifetime employment for him. Despite the lifetime guarantee, a year and a half later, Earl resigned from Sprint because he felt that Sprint could not deliver the kind of customer-centric service that his customers were used to from Hogan & Associates. Now, that's what I call principles!!

As I interviewed these men, three central themes began to emerge that I thought had a perfect parallel with success at P&G. When I talk about the last two (ROI and Passion) you will hopefully say, "Oh, yah! That makes sense", and hopefully my examples will help you see a direct correlation to your role within P&G. The very first theme that I found may surprise you, because it surprised me. What I found was that all three of these men were trying to de-commoditize their businesses. Now, you might say that is just differentiation, and certainly they were trying to differentiate from their competition, but de-commoditization goes much deeper.

De-commoditization

De-commoditization. Don't bother looking that up in your Funk & Wagnal's dictionary. It does not exist, although that has never stopped anyone from P&G before, so I'm not going to let it stop me now. I'll even give you a definition for it, but first I want to talk a little about what a "commodity" is, and why P&G does not want any of our businesses to be considered one.

You have probably all heard of the commodities market where you can buy or sell things like oil, soybeans, sugar, orange juice and even pork bellies. The prices for these goods are set globally and are pretty much dictated by supply and demand. The idea is that cotton is cotton, wheat is wheat and corn is corn. There's not much you can do to these products to add value, so the price can be set at a very broad level. In fact, if you did look up "commodity" in the dictionary you would probably find something like this:

> Commodity - 1: an economic good: as a product of agriculture or mining of commerce especially when delivered for shipment 2: something useful or valued: **3: a good or service whose wide availability typically leads to smaller profit margins and diminishes the importance of factors (as brand name) other than price**

I have bolded and underlined the key definition above to make my point. Commodity – a good or service whose wide availability typically leads to smaller profits and diminishes the importance of factors, such as brand names, other than price. With brand names like Tide and Crest and Pampers, you can all understand why P&G does not like the idea of having any of our products treated like a commodity. This is why we work so hard at de-commoditizing our brands. What I was surprised to find is that all three of these businesses were also very involved in this same practice. So, let's define this practice of de-commoditization.

> De-commoditization – The practice of adding value to a product or service so as to avoid having that product or service treated as a commodity.

Let's start with Marketplace Grill, where, as you can imagine, Dave Godwin has the highest likelihood of being treated like a commodity. After all, a chicken breast is a chicken breast is a chicken breast, right? So why will we sometimes pay as little as $3.00 for that chicken breast dinner and sometimes we'll pay as much as $20 for it? Trust me, Dave wants more than $3.00, but he knows he has to earn his way to charge more and still have his customers feel good about it. I think the best way to describe how Dave feels about de-commoditization is to show you his mission statement.

> Marketplace Grill Mission Statement – To provide our guests with an exceptional dining experience, including food prepared with the best ingredients and service provided by a professional and well developed staff.

This allows Dave to charge more than $3.00 for his chicken breast. I have been to the Marketplace Grill, and I can tell you that I will gladly pay more to eat my chicken breast there. The first thing Dave does is to make his chicken breast different. He adds his best seasoning and prepares it perfectly. He also delivers that chicken breast to me with great service and in a pleasant atmosphere. A chicken breast is not a chicken breast at the Marketplace Grill. Of course, I'm just using a chicken breast as the example here. At Marketplace Grill, Dave applies the same preparation and service to all of his menu items, but I was really surprised to find that

Mike Rethlake was also practicing de-commoditization at his service station.

In the service station business, you might think that a car part is a car part and an hour of labor is an hour of labor no matter where you go, but Mike understands that is not the case. Mike knows that the amount of business he can get and keep and even how much he can charge for his services depends on TRUST. If you are anything like me, you probably feel completely at the mercy of the mechanic when you take your car in to get it serviced. If I could find a mechanic that I felt I could trust, I would take my car there every time. I'm not even sure I would care or even know what a fair cost for parts and labor are, but if I was confident that I wasn't getting cheated (having work done that doesn't need to be done), I would be a satisfied customer.

Mike works hard to build that trust. First, he has developed some standards that he applies to his business that are all about building trust. The most important standard is, "Treat our customers like we would like to be treated." I've seen Mike at work applying this standard, and I can tell you that he works hard at it. He has told me stories about cars that he had worked on for hours, but couldn't find the problem, and how he returned them to the owners with no charge asking them to bring it back when it started acting up again. And they do! He

De-commoditization – adding value to any product or service.

makes it a point to oil squeaky doors also, for free. We all know how a squeaky door can drive us crazy. Mike says that about 75% of doors squeak and he "unsqueaks" them for free. It takes very little time and a few cents worth of oil, but it makes a big impression on his customers. Mike does all of this to build trust with his customers. He learned it from the best, his dad, who said, "Quality service offsets price every time." Gee, I think Vern could have worked for us.

At Hogan and Associates, they tried to differentiate themselves from their competition by making money for their customers. The advertising industry is rife with awards. Which commercials are most creative? Which ad got the highest readership? The list goes on and on. I think we have all watched a commercial on TV and commented on how creative or funny or touching it was, and then asked, "What product was that commercial advertising?" At Hogan and Associates, they made their customers sales and profits THE major focus of their results, and their customers loved it. Maybe there should be an award for that!

If we were owners, de-commoditization is a practice that we would participate in. We would want our brands names to stand for quality and trust, and we would be rewarded by our customers as a result. But, as salespeople, we should be participating in de-commoditization also. After all, a salesperson is NOT just a salesperson. We need to continually be setting ourselves apart from our competition. Anyone can sell brands to our customers, the retailers, but the good ones will go the extra mile providing error free work, better analysis, more accurate predictions and recommendations that will better help them reach their goals. If we are different – better than our competition, we will be rewarded for it. So, work on the business fundamentals better than the other guy, and do it with more persistence and empathy, and in the end you will win for yourself and for the company. Don't become a commodity. Be different. Add value!!

Return on Investment

The fact that individual business owners are concerned about return on investment (ROI) is probably not a shock to any of you, but this is an area where we can sometimes get a little lax. Procter & Gamble is a huge company with a rich supply of resources (money, people, facilities), and in this environment we can all forget to be as demanding as we should when we use those resources. When I started with the company I was encouraged to treat the company's money "like it was my own." Whether it is for expenses or for investment, I think the company would still encourage us to do the same, so before we apply this rule to our jobs let's take a look at some of the tough choices that some individual owners had to make.

Under the Marketplace Grill umbrella, Dave Godwin also had a restaurant called Brioso Brazil. This was a very high-end, Brazilian steak house that offered its customers as much as they would like of a wide variety of very high quality meat. Customers had a card at their table with a green side and a red side. As long as the green side was up, servers continued to bring skewers of delicious meat to your table.

This high profile restaurant in Northwest Arkansas was a jewel in the Marketplace Grill Company crown. Dave took a lot of pride in this restaurant, but a time came when Dave had to make a decision. Lease signing time came and while Brioso was doing OK financially, and it was a source of pride for Dave, the new lease put them in the red or at least very close to it. For Dave, whose income depends on the profitability of the Marketplace Grill Company, it was a no brainer. Even though he liked the volume and liked being the owner of an upscale restaurant in Northwest Arkansas, he would not sign the new lease and the Brioso Brazil restaurant would cease to exist.

Southside Marathon is constantly challenged with decisions on how to equip the station. Should they put a canopy above their gas pumps? Should they buy the latest engine diagnostic equipment for the service area? Should they put in a fourth bay with a car lift so that they can do more oil changes, lube jobs and tire work while the other bays are used on more serious automobile maladies? I've literally seen Mike struggle with each of these decisions, and the outcome always came down to, "What are we going to get for that investment." Mike will diligently do a forecast of incremental volume and profit that he would expect from any such move. He religiously includes improved customer satisfaction or trust into his

> # Spend, invest and save the company's money as if it were your own.

formula before he decides, but he never puts pride or an elevated personal status into the equation.

At Hogan & Associates, Earl lives and dies by his P&L. In fact, Earl hired an independent accounting firm to keep him honest and provide a monthly P&L statement for his company. Whether it was salaries or rent or office supplies, Earl wanted to know if his percentages were in line with what a profitable business should deliver. When considering new clients, he projected the volume and profit that they would bring in compared to the expenses that these new clients would force him to incur. If the numbers did not add up, he would forgo the new clients business rather than try to cut too many corners and jeopardize the quality of the service his company was known to deliver.

We need to act in the same way. While P&G supplies an environment of abundant resources, we need to act as if we are operating in an environment of scarcity. We need to make sure that pride and personal gain has nothing to do with our decisions, and ask the question that all of these owners ask of themselves, "What will the COMPANY get for this investment?" Whether it is KBD or SIB funds or expenses, we need to treat the company's money as if it were our own. Now, I think I should make a plug for some training that I know is available through our SCD (Sales Capability Development) group. It is called "P&G Money Flow" map training. It will teach you the fundamentals about how P&G makes money and how you can help the company make more. It will help you see and act like an owner. If you haven't taken this training, I would suggest that you call your Regional Trainer and find out how you can get involved.

Personal Passion

When I first started to look at these three men to find the common threads that had lead to their success, I noticed their work ethics. Mike still opens and closes the station many days, Dave works incredible hours and of course is at work every time we go out to dinner, and Earl seems to never stop working. He is up at the crack of dawn and when he was running Hogan and Associates, I have it on good authority that he was the last one to leave the office most evenings. This leads to the conclusion that their common thread was work ethic. But then I noticed that there was something they had in common that drove their work ethic. It was a personal passion for the business they were running.

My first clue of this root cause to these incredible work ethics came during my interview with Dave Godwin. Dave, almost apologetically, indicated that he had built his business around himself, not his personality, but his skills and his principles. I would argue that there is a little of his personality in it as well. The Marketplace Grill is efficient, customer focused, and run with extremely high standards, and this is because Dave is the Owner, and THAT is Dave.

As I looked at Southside Marathon, I found that what it did and how it worked reminded me a lot of Mike Rethlake. What a shock! Southside Marathon is not only a very different business than Marketplace Grill, but it is run very differently and feels very different. Southside Marathon is a very casual place. I almost always hear a new joke when I frequent the station and if it weren't for the blue shirts with their names on them, I would sometimes have a hard time telling the customers from the employees. The customers are often chipping into the levity on an equal level to workers, and that is Mike!

At Hogan and Associates, there was a much more formal atmosphere. People were extremely well dressed. The office furniture was very nice. Meetings were run on a regular schedule and people were on time. No one was more on time, however, than Earl Hogan. The other thing that I noticed about these three businesses is that the people who worked there loved it. The atmosphere in each place was very different, but the people working there were very comfortable. They were comfortable because each business reflected the owner in direction, in principle and in atmosphere, and of course each business was successful. People are comfortable when they know who is in control and they can feel that control throughout the organization.

This principle is also incredibly important at P&G. While there are certain directions that we will all get from the company and certain principles that we need to adhere to, there is plenty of room for you to put your personal touch onto your business. The direction and principles that we receive from the company deliver that sense of security or comfort that the people at Marketplace Grill, Southside Marathon and Hogan and Associates feel within those companies. The personal touch that you give to your business will supply you with a passion for that business that the company desperately wants us all to have.

I have had the opportunity to watch people work on projects that affected my businesses. From my days as a unit manager to my work on the Walmart Team, I've seen people do work that was assigned to them and I've gotten to approve some projects that people proposed to me. Work that was their idea. I can tell you that there is no comparison to the effort, creativity and even the results of those who are working on a project that is of their own creation. First of all, they take the results personally. They attack the project with greater energy, and they are open to try every angle that could bring them success. All of these things add up to the personal passion that any owner feels about his or her own business.

When P&G entrusts us with a business we all need to approach it like we own it. Outside of the general direction and principles that they will supply us for comfort and security, they expect us to bring our own personal passion to our work. We all have our own unique mix of skills and experiences that we need to apply to our labor. There are as many ways to be successful as there are people in the company. Each of us will approach the work differently. We may even decide to have a different focus, but if we all have the personal passion of an owner, we are all more likely to deliver successful results.

Imagine!

Imagine a company comprised of 138,000 owners. 138,000 people relentlessly trying to separate themselves and their products from their competition.   138,000 people who were constantly watching to see if their investments in time and money were returning a proper yield for the company and then repeating those activities that did well and eliminating the ones that did not.   Finally, think of a company with 138,000 owners who were utilizing their own personal strengths, skills, knowledge and experience to positively impact their portion of the company's business.

Now, that's a company that I want to work for, and that can be P&G – if we all act like owners!

Introduction for Leveraging Scale by Dale Pirkle,

Lifetime Achievement winner in 2007

Introduction:

I felt this chapter did a wonderful job of adding clarity to what scale means and why we need to claim it. My experience has been that leveraging scale all comes together at the first moment of truth. When executed properly it produces a rare win, win, win situation between P&G, our retail partners and the community. For example, when we leverage scale promotionally, P&G wins because we maximize our combined efforts into an efficient and successful sales event. Our retail partners realize some of their largest sales weeks of the year along with improved portfolio profit mix. Lastly, the community and shoppers win through attractive pricing on leading brands and because many of these events are linked to charitable causes like Special Olympics, League Against Cancer and St. Jude's Hospital just to name a few. Leveraging scale like this allows us to be true to our values by giving back to the communities where we live.

Leveraging Scale

Chapter 13

Scale, what is it? Why do I want it, and what do I do with it once I get it? While the top managers of most companies know the answers to these questions, usually the rank and file of their workforce does not. This is an issue because, while top management can create some programs, processes, and systems that encourage the application of scale, it is only the rank and file that can execute, exploit and leverage scale to its fullest extent. In order to facilitate the execution of scale, I thought I would devote a chapter to its understanding.

So, let's begin our understanding by answering the first question. What is it? In order to answer this question I took what I thought was the easy route and went to the dictionary. What I found was 10 different definitions of scale, everything from "thin, flat horny plated covering many fishes and reptiles" to "either pan of a balance, or any weighing machine." However, I didn't find any definition that fit P&G's concept of "leveraging scale", but I did find this:

> "To make according to a scale – scale down (or up) to reduce (or increase) according to a fixed ratio."

What I found, as I looked back, was that most of the definitions had to do with size, either measuring it or demonstrating it. That's when I began to understand that what P&G means by leveraging its scale is simply taking advantage of its SIZE. This made total sense to me, but also lead me to the realization that with size comes both blessings (to leverage) and curses (to overcome). I think the best way for me to explain this is through a sports analogy.

Let's take football as an example. There are certain advantages that both large and small players have. Smaller players, like me, tend to be quicker. They are more elusive and difficult to get your hands on, and thus they make great wide receivers and running backs. Larger players have power. They are usually stronger and more difficult to push around so they tend to make great interior linemen. That makes sense, right?

Now, you don't see many small players with quickness playing on the line in the NFL, because despite their natural quickness, they can't make up

> ## Size brings both blessings (to Leverage) and curses (to overcome)

for the sheer size and strength that the other NFL linemen were blessed with. You do, however, see larger and larger wide receivers at all levels in football. This is because size is not really a detriment to a wide receiver. If a large man can develop the same kind of quickness that a small man has, then his size becomes an additional benefit. The great wide receivers now and in the future are going to be men who can blend the quickness that used to be reserved for smaller players with the power that can comes with size. These are the players that are destined for the Hall of Fame, and that is what P&G wants and HAS to be! We must remember, however, that while size will impair speed in both individuals and companies, it does not automatically incorporate strength or power. For large people and companies, agility and power are both things that need to be earned.

P&G, no doubt, has size. This year we will be the largest consumer goods company in the world with about $75 billion in sales. With this size, however, can come a lack of agility, just as it does in sports. Big people in sports tend to be slower and big companies can get bogged down in bureaucracy and complexity. Since P&G competes with many smaller, non-global, single category competitors that can be very nimble in their much smaller worlds, we need to eliminate any complexity or bureaucracy that reduces our deftness. I was encouraged at this year's annual CBD meeting (2007) to hear that our top management was seriously addressing this issue. They clearly want us to be the huge, agile wide receiver of the business world.

To be GREAT, however, we still need to take advantage of (leverage) our size. If we don't, we'll just be the big wide receiver that goes down with an arm tackle. We won't be great. We'll just be average, and that is not good enough for us. We need to leverage the POWER that comes with our size. Speed and agility along with power will carry us to excellence, which will lead to magnificent returns for our shareholders.

So, how do we leverage our size or scale? There are many ways, but I have found that the people who best understand the power of our scale are the people who don't have it. Smaller companies, who look from the outside at our size and scale, fully understand the advantages that our scale COULD bring to THEIR businesses, and they are just hoping that we don't ever figure out how to fully leverage it. Their biggest fear is our most fervent desire, and that is that we will match their agility AND discover the power of our own scale. So, to explain the advantages of our size and scale, let's imagine that we are a small, one category, one country manufacturer, and let's try to think of all the ways that P&G's scale would drive us crazy.

Total Delivered Cost

P&G's advantages would start with manufacturing and delivering those finished goods to the retailers. The manufacturing process includes the purchase of raw materials that actually go into products (active ingredients), plastic bottles to contain the products, cardboard boxes to ship them in, tape, glue, etc. The suppliers of all of these materials offer a better price to larger customers and are certainly more engaged with them to make sure that these supplies flow uninterrupted to them.

> **Our competition's biggest fear is our most fervent desire...that we will match their agility AND discover the power of our scale.**

My company is a manufacturer of Hair Care products that does about $50 million of business and operates in most of North America. I think that I am a pretty big deal, however I am dwarfed by the P&G's $6.0 billion (estimate) global Hair Care revenues. That would mean that P&G should pay less for their materials and should be less likely to have their supply lines interrupted in case of shortages. But the advantages don't stop there. P&G's business is so huge that most of their business is shipped in full truckloads. A full truck for most of my customers is a Subaru pickup. The bottom line is, not only does it cost less for P&G to manufacture their Hair Care products, but they can also get that product to their customers more cost effectively. If P&G does a good job at leveraging these advantages, my only choices are to:

1. Raise the prices of my product.
2. Compromise my product with less effective but cheaper ingredients, or
3. Make up for these costs by reducing my marketing support.

These are all bad choices, and my real hope is that P&G just doesn't take advantage of their size. Beyond manufacturing and distributing goods, the last point above brings up a whole other area where I must compete with P&G, and that is in marketing support. I wish there was better news in this area, but unfortunately, the disadvantages keep piling up.

Marketing Support

After we have the manufacturing and distribution processes figured out (as best we can) we need to SELL our products to our customers and consumers. As you might guess, again P&G can have a huge advantage. First, their volume allows P&G to have a virtual army of people selling the retailers' headquarters. And, unfortunately for me, they haven't just created an army of sales types, which would be tough enough for me to compete with, but they have created a mass of multi-skilled support teams to service their customers. These multi-talented teams can supply quality marketing concepts, logistical savings and shopper insights to the retailers. Sheer numbers of people would be a big enough problem for me to fight, but this "full service" approach makes it impossible. My only hope is that these teams won't figure out how to work together. Hopefully they will spend their time in mini "turf wars" and won't figure out how to unleash the power of their multi-functional teams.

As if these highly skilled teams are not enough, they have multiple, massive high reach brands to work with. Where I have single brand, simple merchandising ideas to offer, P&G can offer multi-brand, regimen sale concepts and shopper solution ideas. In Hair Care for example, where I can offer a simple Shampoo promotion, they can put together a Shampoo, Conditioner, Styling Aids and even Hair Color regimen. Their regimen concepts can deliver more volume, appeal to more shoppers and even balance out their profit mix, which used to be my one glimmer of hope to compete.

P&G actually has a number of these little regimen packages they can offer like featuring Toothpaste with Toothbrushes or Dental Floss, or combining Detergent with Fabric Softeners or putting Diapers and Wipes together. These combinations of brands are very attractive to retailers for all the reasons mentioned above, but when they create themes that bring three or four of these regimens together into 15 to 20 brand mega events, it is really a killer for me. Imagine trying to compete with a promotional concept that can boast that at least one of their brands can be found in virtually every home in America. The cost for me to even try to compete is absolutely stifling.

And, of course, they also have an advantage in creating demand for their products. As with the manufacturing process, P&G is so huge that it gets the best costs available when they go to advertise their products. Whether they are buying TV time or newspaper or magazine space, their costs per impression should be the lowest. My only hope is that with all of this potential scale advantage, P&G doesn't figure out how to leverage it.

Now that we have all had a chance to view P&G from the outside, let's get back to reality.

The Bottom Line

The bottom line is that our competitors are all hoping that we won't figure out this "power plus agility" equation, however, for us to succeed, that is exactly what we have to do. We have all heard much discussion recently within the company about eliminating complexity and non value added work. All of us need to help the company identify those activities and make sure they get eliminated. As we have been told, when we see waste and bureaucracy we need to stand up and say, "I'm as mad as hell, and I'm not going to take it any more." We need to be quick and nimble to compete with those smaller, single country companies that move fast more naturally.

> **Power plus Agility is the goal of leveraging Scale**

We also need to leverage the power that comes with our size, or we will suffocate under our own massive weight. This is not a choice anymore.

We have to be nimble to compete in the market place, and we must leverage the power that comes with our size or simply suffer from the stifling complexity that comes with it. The good news is, we have ample opportunities to unleash the POWER in our scale.

1. Buying Power – On our teams, when we are buying time or material or anything else, we need to make sure we are getting the very best price, as our scale demands.
2. Logistical Power – We need to figure out how to take advantage of all the volume that we sell and minimize our shipping costs in new in unique ways. The Sam's Team double stack approach for our Paper products is a great example.
3. People Power – We need to fully leverage the talent and experiences of our people. We must remember that we are one company and one team and our goal is to win vs. our competition, like Lever Bros. and Colgate. When we work together like that, we win.
4. Brand Power – We need to bring our brands together in ways that our competition either can't or won't. We need to sell regimens where we have them and mega events that no one can touch. Where we have a unique advantage like this, we need to exploit it.

If we do not do this, our size becomes a burden. It will actually get in our way and reduce the likelihood of our success. If we CAN do this, however, we will be combining the AGILITY that normally comes to smaller companies with the POWER that can come with size and scale. We will be like the 300 pound wide receiver that runs a 4.4 second forty yard dash (for you non-football fans, that is really fast!). In other words, we will be huge and nimble, and that will enable us to deliver Hall of Fame results and the kind of returns that our shareholders (like all of us) expect and deserve.

Introduction for Final Tips by Mark Wellman,
In loving Memory of Kenny Shields, Director HHN,
Walmart Customer Team

Introduction:

*This chapter is focused on ensuring that you have the right balance in your work and personal life. You want to be exceptional in your job, but you don't want it to **define** you. Perhaps no one embraced and embodied the skill of balance better than Kenny Shields. He managed over $6 Billion in sales of Procter & Gamble Household Needs business with Walmart, while maintaining rich relationships with his family, community, church and enumerable friends. Even with the responsibilities of this large business, Kenny devoted time to be the President of the Big Brothers – Big Sisters chapter of Northwest Arkansas. Also, he coached his sons' baseball and basketball teams, while being an active follower and fan of his boys' hockey, tennis and golf teams.*

Kenny believed in the power of love in all aspects of his life and encouraged others by saying, "You have to LOVE what you do! You also need to LOVE the people you work with on a daily basis. Great families and friendships are rooted in love. Great teams have to be also!" Though Kenny passed away from this Earth too soon for all of us, we are uplifted in knowing that his faith will bring him eternal peace and that he lived life to the fullest. He was and continues to be a role model on how to be a successful manager of life.

Final Tips

Chapter 14

Family, Friends, Faith &Fitness

I just love sales people, don't you? Sales "types" tend to be much more social. The really good ones are instinctively trying to build relationships as soon as they meet you, so they tend to be good listeners. They are hard workers and very goal driven so they are great to have as part of any team, whether it is inside the workplace our outside. So, if you are a natural sales type, congratulations. You've got a lot going for you, but there are some watch-outs with these blessings that you need to be aware of. In this last chapter, I hope to give you some tips that will improve not only your performance, but your life.

I have been told many times in my life that my greatest strength can also be my biggest weakness. For example, my tenacity can be a great quality when it drives me to push harder and reach a goal that I might have otherwise missed. It can also be a huge roadblock when I don't know when to give up and look for compromise. One quality that almost all sales types have, as mentioned above, is that we are very goal oriented and driven. Now, this quality, by itself, is a good thing and drives these people to reach the goals they set for themselves or even the goals that are set FOR them. However, when you combine this quality with a sales career, the results can be toxic.

In sales, there is always a number that you are chasing. In fact, today there are many numbers that we track and forecast which are signs of whether we are on target to hit THE big number. Every company for example, especially P&G, is interested in the ROI (return on investment) that their salespeople get from their merchandising funds. It is an indicator of whether the Sales function is getting the best bang for their dollar. In other words, it is an indicator, collectively, if they will hit the BIG number. Every company is concerned about the shares that they have in all of their categories. In the end, however, what every company wants from sales is - sales.

> **The "sales" personality combined with the "sales" career can create a toxic situation**

Whether it is dollars or cases or ounces or units, or all of the above, they want sales. And, they would like you to be able to tell them what you are going to sell, before you sell it, and then SELL it.

So, in sales you start every year chasing a big number and you are constantly tracking a variety of numbers to tell you how you are doing. You will track your progress on a monthly or weekly basis, and if you are lucky enough to work on the Walmart Team, you will track it on a daily, if not hourly, basis. The chase and the tracking never end. In fact, on the Walmart Team we used to celebrate after work on June 30th (the end of our fiscal year) as the "no number" evening. We would have just delivered (hopefully) our last year's number and we wouldn't have to start chasing the next year's number until the next morning. This, of course, was just a charade, since we had all started chasing next year's number, months and even years before. But it was a break we needed to take in an attempt to maintain our sanity.

This is where the job and the personality can get toxic. The spotlight and the chase and the desire to succeed can cause some sales people to neglect other aspects of their life such as their health and even their family. What everyone needs in their life, particularly sales people, is balance. The good news is that the answer to our need for balance is all around us. I simply call it the "4 F's", Family, Friends, Fitness and Faith. It will take some effort and some discipline, but in the end, focus on these areas will not only improve your life, but probably your results in your job as well. Let me tell you the ins and outs of the "4 F's".

Friends

A friend in need is a friend indeed. A friend will never fail you. You can't have too many friends. You have all probably heard these sayings or some like them, and they are all true. It is hard to overemphasize the importance of friends in your life. Your friends can be a needed distraction from the grind of your working life. They can be the support you need at critical points in your life, and they can keep you accountable and be an encouragement at the same time. So, if they are so important, where do you find them and how do you GET them?

You will find potential friends all around you, and I have found that I have

A friend in need is a friend indeed!

many layers of friends. Brenda, my wife, and I have always had five to six couples that I would define as our close friends. That matches up with the sitcom "Friends" number. I'm not sure the creators of that series where trying to make a philosophical comment with that number, but that feels about right for the inner circle. As I look back at that "inner circle", I have found that the source of those friends early in our married life was the people that we worked with. Once we had children, almost all of our core friends seemed to be somehow connected to them. But you must choose these friends carefully. The Bible even suggests this in Proverbs 18:24, where it says,

"A man of many companions may come to ruin,

But there is a friend who sticks closer than a brother"

You can say this about all of your friends, but particularly about your inner circle. For these friends, you not only want to be socially compatible and have some common interests, but they also need to be people that you can trust. These are the people that you may need to lean on or that may want to lean on you. They need to be a special breed. Choose them carefully. By the way, these core friends don't necessarily have to live close by. We have what I consider to be close friends that live hundreds of miles away that we see a few times a year, but they still qualify as "core" friends.

I would suggest that it is also important to have a little distraction from your work-a-day world. Hobbies are a great source for these kinds of friends, and if you don't have some sort of a hobby, it is a sign that your personality and your job requirements are getting toxic. I have a youth Bible study that I have run for 13 years now. I work with a group called AAO that works with the University of Arkansas and with the youth in Northwest Arkansas, and I play a little basketball (my wife would say I play constantly, but that's not true). All of these activities are great distractions from my everyday work and they supply me with great friends. Some of these friends may make it into your inner circle, but most will just be social friends that you will have contact with when you are in their particular sphere and an occasional dinner. These kinds of friends are still extremely important to your health and well being, so I would still apply the Biblical direction for these choices and choose them wisely. They should be good people and have consistent values with you and even with your core friends so that they could be easily mixed together occasionally. I probably have 20 or 30 of these kinds of friends (although I don't want to set a benchmark that is too low here) and they are all a great blessing in my life.

Finally, I think we all need some sort of accountability group. This is a very specialized group that you can meet with regularly to discuss the deeper issues in your life and to get counsel. Some of your core group could be part of this group also, but not necessarily, and certainly not your entire core group. For the past 20 years or so, I have always been part of an accountability or encouragement group. Some people call these "E-Teams". For me, these groups have been connected to my church, and we do Bible studies, we pray for each other and we talk about the issues in our lives. As you might guess, this group needs to be trusted to keep information VERY confidential, so the Biblical direction to choose them wisely certainly applies here. For me, I have only been in one of these groups at a time and the number has varied from three to about 10 people. Again, the Bible encourages this kind of friendship in Proverbs 27:6, where it says,

> **Your inner circle, social and Accountability friends all need to share your core values.**

> "Wounds from a friend can be trusted,

> But an enemy multiplies kisses."

This really speaks to the accountability part of this particular group. This group will not be afraid to tell you when you are messing up. They will tell you and hold you accountable to change, but they will also keep it confidential. Members of this group need very special qualifications like wisdom, discretion, trust, empathy, and strength of character.

Each of these groups offers a particular benefit and the members of these groups have particular requirements. Let me give you a quick recap.

Classification	Source	Requirements	#	Benefits
Core Friends	Work, Children	Compatible, consistent with core values, Supportive	5-10	Support, daily to weekly contact, weekend entertainment
Social (Good Distractions)	Hobbies, Other Interests	Consistent with core values, different walk of life, Fun!	10-20	Fun, escapism, accomplishment - work (but for a different purpose)
Accountability	Church, work, other interest groups	Wisdom, discretion, trust, empathy and strength of character	3-10	Real accountability, improvement of character, counsel

Now, I have hundreds of acquaintances, and those are great to have also. They can be helpful to you or your friends or your family at any time and vice versa, you can be helpful to them, but these would not fall in the description of friends as I have defined above.

Finally, how do you acquire these friends? I think Ralph Waldo Emerson said it best, "The only way to have a friend is to BE a friend." In some ways, I wish there were more to acquiring a friend. This sounds too simple. But in reality, this is an arduous task. This small definition implies a significant amount of give and take on your part, with the emphasis on "GIVE", and it applies to all of the groups above. For core friends and Accountability groups it can take years to develop that kind of interaction and even for good "distraction" friends it can take months to accomplish, but what I can tell you is – GIVE, and the blessings that you will receive in return will be more than worth the effort.

Faith

I feel that I need to start this section off with a bit of a disclaimer. P&G is not a faith based company. We do not sell Bibles or the Koran or any other religious material. I do, however, consider P&G to be a faith friendly company. I believe the company understands the positive influence that most of the world religions can have on the people who work within it.

To quote Randy Alcorn in his book, Heaven, "Anthropological evidence suggests that every culture has a God-given, innate sense of the eternal – that this world is not all there is." I think this explains why so many people around the world have a strong sense of spirituality, and that sense is very personal and can have a very powerful influence on our lives. Most often, this sense of spirituality manifests itself in a participation in one of the world's great religions. Sometimes it is just a sense of awe of nature, its complexity and simplicity at the same time. Whatever that sense of spirituality is in your life, I encourage you to embrace it because it will give you a deeper sense of purpose and direction for you life.

Virtually every religion has its own "Great Book" that gives its believers both purpose and direction. Whether it is the Bible, the Koran, the Talmud, the Tipitaka (Buddhism), the Vedas (Hinduism) the Book of Mormon or another, they all suggest that honesty, integrity, generosity, etc. are good things and this behavior will enhance life here on earth and even after.

If you are a person that participates in one of these great religions, I encourage you to embrace it. Your faith WILL give you purpose and direction. If you follow your faith, you will be a better person; you will be more content, happier, more complete and even more successful and a better employee for P&G. Even if you do not align with any religion at all, I encourage you to explore and embrace "your" sense of spirituality to discover your deeper purpose and direction.

Bonus Tip - Whatever you do, do it with all your heart

I had to put this little tip in. It is one of the things that I like to think I did well. This idea actually comes from Christian Scripture. In Colossians 3:23, it says, "Whatever you do, work at it with all of your heart as for the Lord, not for men." This gives all of our best efforts quite a higher calling, doesn't it!

This is very closely related to my "Persistence" chapter, where I was described as a wire haired terrier with a tennis ball. I've also been told that I only have one speed, full speed. I know that I'm not very good at "letting" other people beat me at anything. You can ask my wife. We have often played tennis together on vacation and I just can't LET her win. Not that she hasn't beaten me, but I never LET her win.

My personality has gone a little beyond the Biblical charge, and when you do that, it can be irritating to other people at times. However, doing your best at all times is something a little different and much more effective. Doing your best leaves room for easing up on your wife because it remembers that the goal in this case is to enjoy the time together, not to win a silly game of tennis. It also leaves room for compromise in a business situation since it knows that the goal isn't to win, but the goal is to move forward. In fact, this attitude takes the positives of persistence and gives it a higher purpose.

Fitness

As I stated earlier, Sales and sales people can develop a toxic relationship. To be the very best, you need to be smart and you need to be strategic. You need to be able to communicate and inspire and lead other people. However, in sales, if you are not goal oriented or results focused (or however you want to describe this quality) you will probably not be successful and you certainly will not be happy, because that IS the job. The job involves a constant, moving target, which, when combined with your relentlessly driven personality, can literally lead you to an early grave. To avoid an early and unexpected departure from this life, you will need to take care of yourself both physically and mentally.

My advice, first, recognize the potential dangers. Second, put a plan in place to address them and approach this plan with the same discipline that you do your job. Let me give you some areas to consider and some ideas, from experience, on how to approach those areas.

Your Physical Health

Your health is a particularly important area not to neglect because the stress of the job and your personality can, literally, kill you. It doesn't have to cost a lot of money and it doesn't have to take a lot of time, but it WILL take discipline. The good news is, if you are a "sales" type person, you will have the discipline to pull this off. Here are my recommendations of what you should do:

-**If you don't work out now, you need to start**. This could be walking or running or riding a bike. You don't need to have a personal trainer or belong to a health club. The roads, the parks and hotel workout rooms are free. Use them! You can lift weights too, but don't confuse that with aerobic exercise which is good for your heart.

-**You need to work out regularly**. Three to five times a week for 20 to 60 minutes of continuous aerobic activity at 60-90% of your maximum heart rate – minimum!

-**Impose your will on others**. If someone wants to work all day and then meet at dinner and eat and drink all night, tell them that it will have to wait until you get your workout in. A late dinner won't ruin anything. If meetings are planned that don't allow you to get in a workout, give them feedback. They need to fix that and you can be part of the fix!

-When you travel, make your workout clothes be the first thing you pack. Think about it until it's a habit, and then you won't have to think about it again.

-Go to the doctor. The company has great benefits. Utilize them. You should especially make sure to get regular check ups. Doctors can do wonderful things for you, if you go to them. They can't do anything for you if you don't.

Your Mental Health

When God created this planet, he placed man in the middle of a veritable feast. Man's life could be both wonderful and wondrous. This feast offers us all elaborate complete courses with an infinite variety of tastes and textures and aromas. God doesn't, however, demand that you experience the entire banquet. He offers it to us, but if you choose to only go to the salad bar at every meal and only eat lettuce with no dressing, you can do that. It's a little sad, but sometimes that actually happens, and in the end, the life that limits its experiences limits its joy as well.

I only write this because the "sales" personality and the "sales" job can have the effect of sending us all to the salad bar everyday. We "sales" types can get so focused on the chase for both cases and success that we inadvertently ignore all of the other wonderful possibilities that are all around us. So that you don't get to the end of a lifelong salad bar only to discover that you could have had filet mignon and

> **Get to the entree and dessert cart of life – read, study and get involved!**

lobster and turkey and sweet potatoes (I'm starting to get hungry), I am going to implore you now to force yourself to experience the other possibilities early and often. Some people are more natural at this, but if you are not, here are some things you can do to expose you to some of the other dishes life has to offer.

Read – Yes, you can read <u>Built to Last</u> and <u>Good to Great</u> and other good business related books, but you can't stop there. Read some novels (I love Clive Custler and Grishom and Patterson). Read some history. Read others opinions. I read <u>It Takes a Village</u>, not because I agree with Hillary Clinton, in fact quite the opposite. I read it to understand how she thinks. All of this will expose you to other opinions and other unique and interesting ideas and different ways to express those ideas. Books are some of the great side dishes of life. Get in line and enjoy.

Get involved – There are hundreds, if not thousands, of great causes that need your time and talents. Whether it is the elimination of some disease or the welfare of those more vulnerable AND the future of our country (children) or defending our natural resources, you can improve the world we live in and reap some personal benefits as well like:

> -**Give yourself some perspective**. Sometimes we begin to think that "everyone is looking at me" or that we are center of the universe. Involvement will remind you that there is much more out there than just little old us. It will also let you know how blessed you are.

> -**Meet some wonderful people**. Think of the people that are involved in your community. They aren't perfect, but they tend to be vital, energetic and interesting. They are fun to be around and can teach you much.

> -**It can bring you real joy**. There is nothing like working hard at something you REALLY believe in, and see the results of your efforts; a changed life or an improved situation. It can be extremely satisfying.

This can also add some real meat to your life. Many people continue to work for these causes after their work life is over and find as much challenge and more satisfaction than they ever did in their business life. I would counsel you not to wait until you retire, but get started now and reap the benefits for as long as possible.

Study – This is different from just reading. "Study" implies a careful examination of a subject or issue that goes beyond just awareness. It leads to a deeper understanding and knowledge of the subject. I would always encourage a study of the Bible because there is SO much wisdom contained in it and it IS an inexhaustible study. Some people have spent their entire lives studying it only to find that it only shows them how little they know. I long to do this study even more aggressively than I do today. You can study history or philosophy or politics (ugh). No matter what you study it will expose you to more of the feast of life.

This will all lead to a strong mind and a strong body that will be able to withstand the rigors of a sales job combined with a sales personality. Without this focus on your physical and mental wellbeing, your life will certainly not be as fulfilling as it could, and could even be disastrous. Take care of your body AND your mind!

Family

A wise man once told me (in fact many wise people have told me) that they have never heard of a person on their death saying that they wished they had spent more time working. They may say that they wished they had spent more time traveling or reading, but most say that they wished they had spent more time with their families. I'm not on my death bed, but I can already say that I wish that I had spent more time with my family.

> **You should cherish both the family you are born into and the one you help create.**

Most of us in life will be blessed with two families, the one we are born into and the one we create with our spouses. Both should be cherished. The family that I was born into happened to be a great one. My mother and father had seven children (I was the youngest), and they managed to get us all to adulthood with just minor cuts and bruises, but also with some pretty good values. We have made an effort to stay together, despite the fact that we currently live in five different states that extend from the east to the west coast. We have written family chain letters. We visit each other whenever we can. We call each other often and now, as our children get married, we try to make each event a family reunion. I encourage you to do the same. Blood is thicker than water and there is something about the support you can get from your family and the understanding they have of your life that you can't get anywhere else. If you are lucky enough to come from a family like mine, this will be easy. If not, it may be more difficult, but I encourage you to take the mending step. You will be blessed for it.

In the family that Brenda and I created together, I wish I could say that I have no regrets. But I do. When I was younger, and my daughters were growing up, I was working hard and playing hard and providing for the family. When we lived in California, I was traveling four days a week, working hard and when I got home, I was trying to recover from my difficult work schedule, which didn't include time with my daughters. There are two incidents that made me realize the errors of my ways.

The first incident involved "airport presents". When I started my job in California, my daughters were quite young. They were still playing with dolls and playing "grocery store" in our garage. Even though I was on the road four days a week, I believed I was being an incredibly thoughtful father because I always brought my daughters something home for them after my trip. Of course, I was usually too rushed at the airport to pick them up actual "airport presents", so I would always bring them home the little shampoo bottles and soap bars from the hotels where I had stayed. In the beginning, they loved them. My presents became part of their inventory in their garage/grocery store.

Then, after a couple of years, I came home one Friday and proudly announced that I had a surprise for my two daughters, when my oldest said to my youngest, "It's no big deal. It's just soap." That was when I realized that my daughters were growing up, and I was missing it. In that same year, I took a week off and just stayed home to rest and "be with my family!" On Monday morning I felt like I was in front of a moving conveyor belt, but I had no idea what we were making or what my job was. I kept hearing things like, "Dad, we always do this on Monday", followed by, "This is what we always do on Tuesday." Substitute a different day, and that is what I was hearing every day.

This is when I realized that I was missing out on most of my family's life. I would like to tell you that I did a complete 180 in my husband/father role, but I didn't. I made slow progress from there on and I think I turned out OK, but I missed SO MUCH! And, I can never get it back. My counsel to you is to know that your job and your personality will try to pull you away from your family, and you will have to make an effort to prevent that. Get involved with your spouse and your children's lives. You will NOT regret it. You can thank me later for all of the little moments that you *don't* miss.

In Closing

Life is uncertain. There are infinite possibilities, challenges, joys and regrets that we will each face. One thing that we can all agree on (at least most of us) is that we only get one ride. There are no "do overs" or mulligans on life. Also, it is not about the destination, but it is about the ride. When we get to the destination, we all want to make sure we have made the most of the ride. We want to make sure that we didn't miss any possibilities just because we weren't looking or because we made bad choices.

I'm hoping that this book will help your ride. If you sell for a living, especially consumer products, I hope this book will help you be more successful at it. If you are, that success can give you some joy and a sense of accomplishment and even some resources that can help you enjoy the rest of what life can offer. Once you have that "business" part of your life under control, this last chapter will hopefully help you enjoy the rest of life. We all have one ticket, one ride. My hope is that when you get to your destination you don't have any major regrets. Remember, he who dies with the most toys, still dies. It's not about what you have accumulated; it is about what you have experienced. Experience the entire banquet, not just the salad bar! If this book helps get you to the dessert tray, it was worth the writing.

P.S.

If any of you have seen the classic play or movie Annie, you will probably remember the song "Tomorrow". As Annie struggles with her disappointments of today, she sings, "The sun will come out tomorrow", and "Tomorrow, tomorrow, I love you tomorrow. You're only a day away." While I would always encourage people to look forward to the future, and this is a great song for a Broadway show, it is not a great theme for this last chapter.

The slogan for this chapter is, "Tomorrow is promised to no man (or woman)". TODAY is the operative word for implementing a plan for the 4 F's. Get started TODAY. Go to the doctor to get yourself checked out. Start your new workout program. Get involved with the community and with your family TODAY. I have known too many people who planned to execute the 4 F's tomorrow, but never got the chance to do it. If you only take one piece of counsel from me, let it be that you start your new life of family, friends, faith and fitness today! Yesterday is gone. Tomorrow is promised to no one. TODAY is all you really have to work with.

KEVIN CANFIELD

About the Cover

The original cover was a PowerPoint slide, which I have pictured below. I found this slide in the clip art library about seven years ago when I was looking for an opening slide for a presentation, a slide that could be up on the screen when the buyer came into the room.

I loved this slide. I thought it painted the perfect picture of the partnership that must exist between manufacturers and retailers if both are to succeed in what they do. I started almost every presentation with this slide for the next four years. It became an expectation from my buyers. It also lead to some great discussions about whatever idea I was about to present, or light hearted discussions of who was the retailer and who was the manufacturer on this slide. I always saw myself as the guy on the top, but many of my buyers pointed out that the person on the bottom was carrying a briefcase, which is decidedly synonymous with sales. No matter what the discussion it always left the buyer in a good mood and the ground fertile for selling. So why did we change it?

Both of my daughters, who are in their late 20's now, told me that while the sentiment was nice, the slide itself was a little "old school". So, we decided to modernize it. The original cover had a picture of me and one of my daughters and a fellow P&G employee named Minki Chang. We were pictured in one of P&G's high tech facilities. We all thought that this demonstrated diversity of age, gender and race and would make for a very appealing cover. However, while my daughter was lovely and Minki was Minki, I never liked my picture on the cover. The current cover was actually designed by a professional and is supposed to conjure visions of successful selling. The green color and the money graphics speak to volume and profit while the hands shaking remind us of the agreement needed to complete any sale. Finally, the rippling circles suggest the need to be on target with your plans.

No matter which cover you liked best, I hope you have enjoyed reading the book, and now I hope that just looking at the cover can remind you of the major points that it brings out. Be proud of what you do. Do it well, and lift up the new people in the company who will follow you to drive the stock price for years to come.

Good Selling,

Kevin Canfield

KEVIN CANFIELD

Made in the USA
Charleston, SC
24 January 2015